A Psalmist's Guide to Grief

by E. Anne Weil

Dedication

This book would not be reality without the encouragement and love of a multitude of family and friends. You circled around us and lifted us up with prayer and love in the darkest period of our grief. You danced and sang with joy along with us when we had good news to share. You are brightly shining examples of the Body of Christ, and I am eternally grateful to God for giving us this beautiful glimpse of the love we'll find in heaven.

Introduction

I fought writing this book for several years: I didn't feel
exceptionally qualified to write as an expert on any
spiritual topic. Grief, on the other hand, is something I
am intimately acquainted with; I've lived in its shadow for
over a decade now. My husband and I struggled to have
children. We were able to become pregnant, but we had
ten pregnancy losses - nine before our daughter was born,
and one more miscarriage since then. For over ten years
now, I have struggled to cope with the grief and depression
left in the wake of all that devastation. I have doubted
everything, including God, at some point, and I wonder all
the time if I will ever be whole again – if I will ever not feel
like a failure – if I will ever really be able to face off with
the real depth of my pain and walk away alive.

Maybe you are facing a different kind of loss; we feel
grief over all sorts of losses, and not all them involve the
physical loss of a loved one. We are more adept at
understanding that someone will feel grief when a loved
one dies. We are less aware that you can also grieve the loss
of a job, the loss of a friendship, the dissolution of a
marriage, and even the loss of a dream: we may not
recognize those losses as well, but they are all things that we
will mourn in some way when they are lost. Perhaps you
are single at a stage in life when you had planned to be
married and have a family. Perhaps you thought you'd have
a family by now, but having children is fraught with more
obstacles than answers. There are a lot of things that can
cause us to grieve over our circumstances. I want to

continue to learn how to better grieve as one who has hope – because I do have tremendous hope in Jesus – and to live in that hope as a more healthy and whole person.

When my husband and I revisited the conversation about trying to have another baby, it just ripped all the old scars open into raw and festering wounds once more, and I realized in that moment of fresh pain that grief isn't a single obstacle to overcome but a lifelong journey of healing. I don't know the details of how this journey ends for us, but I know that I am learning to embrace my faith for what it is (and what it isn't). I have learned that just being honest with God is most of the battle in facing my feelings and my grief. I have no magic bullets – just long, arduous work – but in that work you will find God, and you will show him your heart, and you will begin to limp and then to walk and then to run again.

If no one else has told you these words, then you need to know that you are stronger than you realize, and God is bigger than you can imagine; if he is for you, nothing can stand against you, and if you belong to him, he is most assuredly for you. God is for you. The creator of the universe – who holds worlds in his hands and speaks everything into existence – the savior of the world is on your side. He's got you. Let that be your safe place to anchor and weather the storm that seems to surround you at every turn. You are precious to him no matter how you feel and no matter how far and how hard you run.

I ran for a long time. I still attended church somewhat regularly, but I avoided people as much as possible. I was afraid that if I talked to anyone for very long they might discover that I was a fraud – that I, who professed to be a follower of Christ, was struggling to believe that God could be good. What I saw around me were people who had their lives together, who weren't struggling with any tenet of their faith, who must see right through me and realize that I was not what I pretended to be. I quit reading my Bible for months, and I struggled to pray at all; then I began avoiding church altogether because I wanted to yell through half the service that I couldn't believe that anything we sang or prayed or preached was true. I finally realized that I had come to a point where I had to "put up or shut up." If I couldn't believe that God was good, then I couldn't believe anything else about him either. Was I really ready to walk away from God completely?

Almost. I was hurting in ways I had never imagined. I felt like my body had betrayed me, as I had failed to do the one thing my body was specifically designed to do. Everything I read when I did try to study the Bible seemed to condemn me, and I felt a million miles away from God. How could this misery be God's plan for my life? How could terrible people have babies they didn't even want while I abjectly failed? How awful must I be for God to punish me this way? Why should I believe anything?

So I started with "A is A." "A is A" is the ancient Greek philosophical law of identity that states that every thing is the same as itself and different from other things, or, put another way, all things have their own essence with individual characteristics or composition. So, A is A, but A is not B; B is B. In spiritual terms, God had always been the bedrock of my life (my A), so to turn away from that meant starting over from the beginning. I couldn't disbelieve in my life's foundation without deciding what to build on. I knew I couldn't find another religion that would fill that need because I studied other faiths, and many were based on belief in a god, if not the same God I was considering walking away from. I couldn't base my life solely on myself because I was on shaky ground mentally, spiritually, and emotionally, so I was a terrible foundation. I studied math as an exercise in looking at a "pure" science that was unlikely to change based on some new scientific theory (because if Pluto could suddenly not be a planet, nothing was certain in science, either...). Algebra felt like an immutable truth, and it offered a tiny respite from the swirling doubt that threatened to destroy me. Although I solved for A quite a bit in my algebra practice, math wasn't enough to be the A I could begin building on.

I worked up the nerve to really examine my faith from the very first building block. Did I believe that God exists? Yes (A). Did I believe that God is in control of all creation? Yes (B). Did I believe that God is the only good and the only truth? Yes (C). Then I must believe all of him (the whole alphabet!). I must believe that God was still in control of my life, too, as painful as that was to admit. And if I believed God, then I must also act on that faith. I made an effort to get back into a small group Bible study, I joined the choir, and I started reading my Bible most days. My prayer life was still struggling, so I decided to just read a Psalm each day for a while. I switched to a more plain-language translation to change my approach and see the words in a fresh way, and I discovered that the Psalms were very often describing my emotional state of despair. More than that, the psalmists themselves pulled no punches when talking to God about their problems. If they could be honest with God, then maybe I could tell him exactly how I felt, too. I started pouring out everything into a journal, and I began to feel lighter.

The one consistent coping skill that has worked for me is to journal. Writing down all the mess floating around in my head and my heart helps call back into order the chaos all the emotions of grief inspire. I even go old school and keep a paper journal book handy pretty much all the time. Somehow angry clicking on the keyboard isn't as satisfying as carving my angst onto the page with a pen, and the time it takes to handwrite allows me to process my feelings and name them. The act of identifying what I'm feeling and why I'm feeling it gives me power over the emotions and lets me form new thought processes. I don't really ever want to read most of my journal entries again. I'm not sure that I should even keep them; I've even considered burning them. The point is, they allow the emotions that threaten to creep out and cause me to act like a buffoon/jerk to escape safely onto a page without actually kicking anyone in the shins. Maybe you aren't a writer, but you do have some way that lets you express yourself – art or dance or music or running. If you know what your mode of expression is, use it in this walk through the Psalms. If you have no idea what your thing is, write and sketch and see what happens.

The goal here is to hold your doubts and emotions and insecurities up to God and to let him shine through those things into our souls. It won't always feel illuminating. It will often feel painful and shameful. You may not feel like enthusiastically praising God for a while. Those things are all okay to feel. But it's really important to recognize that feelings aren't God's truth. It's also important to recognize that sometimes our feelings are overwhelming, and we may need help beyond what our journals or friends and family can provide. I am a big fan of therapy; please don't be afraid to ask for help if life is feeling too big to handle for a little while. I have spent quality time in a counselor's office, and I will spend more time there as life goes on if I run into more big things.

This book will be organized by topic rather than biblical chapter order, and it's formatted with space to journal in the book if you choose to do so. I find it impossible to write about grief without feeling a bit fractured, with my mind wandering several places at once. That said, journaling tends to bring order out of chaos for me, so I hope you will follow along and find the same moments of calm in studying the Bible and reflecting in the journal space here. (If you are a bibliophile like me and can't stand the thought of writing in a book, get a blank journal or notebook and follow along.) Don't be afraid to skip around through the chapters if you are struggling with a particular stage of grief and want to focus on that topic first. It will help if you do Chapter 1 first just to get the lay of the land, so to speak, but the chapters should stand alone well enough not to feel lost if you skip around.

My prayer for everyone who picks up this book is that God will open your heart to his truth and comfort and perfect peace. I pray that *A Psalmist's Guide to Grief* will be a tool for healing. And I pray that my story will help you to know that you are not alone in grief and that you will have the courage to share your story and encourage someone else in their journey.

"Then Jesus said, 'Come to me, all of you who are weary and carry heavy burdens, and I will give you rest. Take my yoke upon you. Let me teach you, because I am humble and gentle at heart, and you will find rest for your souls. For my yoke is easy to bear, and the burden I give you is light." Matthew 11:28-30 NLT

Table of Contents

Chapter 1 – Be Honest

As we begin to work through our grief and study through the Book of Psalms, you should notice that above all, the psalmists, especially David, are brutally honest before God. David was always described as a man after God's own heart. If David, who is so tenderly loved by God, could be real about his pain and angst, why can't you? And don't even begin to think that David must have been a better person than you could ever be – he committed adultery and murder (you can read all about David's story in the books of 1 Samuel, 2 Samuel and 1 Kings), and God still loved him and blessed him.

It is hard, and maybe just a tiny bit scary, to think of being honest with God. If you grew up going to church like I did, you may have learned that God is to be praised or feared or respected above all, so telling God how you really feel about a situation seems awkward at best and blasphemous at worst. You may have learned formulaic prayers or memorized creeds, and it is difficult, if not impossible, for you to form prayers outside those models. But consider this: God knows your soul more intimately than anyone earth can ever know you. He knows every thought you have, and he still loves you. So let's strip away the facades we show other people and just exist as we are when we talk to God. I have found that when I show God all of me, I more often than not come away with a new and deeper understanding of who God is.

To begin understanding how this looks in practice and how we'll tackle each Psalm, we're going to read Psalm

102. I'm going to quote from the New Living Translation, but use whatever you have and like to read the best.

I really love reading texts in both the New King James Version (NKJV) and the New Living Translation (NLT). I studied Hebrew in college, and I think the NKJV does the best job of translating the mood and song of the poetry. The NLT makes me think better in plain language, which helps me to apply what I'm reading more directly to my life. When I want to look at something from a different perspective, I'll use a Bible app to read through several different translations. Pick a translation that is easily readable to you so that you can understand what you are reading; I firmly believe that God will use any translation of his word when we are faithful to read it and apply it to our lives. Isaiah 40:8 NLT says, *"The grass withers and the flowers fade, but the word of our God stands forever."* Forever means that his truth infuses every faithful translation of the Bible, and he won't let us mere humans stand in the way of his message.

Psalm 102

When I read Psalm 102, I realize that we are all psalmists. We may not all pray in rhyming verse or elegant phrases, but anyone who speaks honestly with God is a psalmist. If you are speaking your heart song, whatever that may be at the moment, and however you may be expressing it, you are a poet in the truest sense of the word. I love reading in the book of Psalms every day because it reminds me to be honest with God. The introduction to Psalm 102 in the New Living Translation reads, *"A prayer of one overwhelmed with trouble, pouring out problems before the Lord."*

How many times have I been there, pouring out my troubles to God? And the overwhelmed author of Psalm 102 lays it all out: *"For my days disappear like smoke, and my bones burn like red-hot coals. My heart is sick, withered like grass, and I have lost my appetite."* Yes!

(Except for the appetite part – I'm a stress eater, and I talk to God about that, too.) God, listen to me and how horrible I feel right now. These are my problems, and I want you to do something about them now! Quite a few psalms go this way; David was very emphatic about what he wanted God to do about his enemies. It obviously doesn't hurt to be very specific with God.

But psalms almost never end with just problem dumping and enemy shaming and to-do lists for God. Even Psalm 102, which purports to be *"a prayer of one overwhelmed with trouble, pouring out problems before the Lord,"* doesn't end with merely pouring out problems. Less than half-way through the dump session, the focus shifts from problems to perfection, *"But you, O Lord, will sit on your throne forever. Your fame will endure to every generation,"* and ends with, *"But you are always the same; you will live forever. The children of your people will live in security. Their children's children will thrive in your presence."*

Wait... What? What happened to all the troubles? You know they didn't just vanish, but they certainly disappeared from view when compared to God. That's the thing I miss sometimes in my moments of being real with God. I tell him my problems, and I tell him what I want him to do about them, but I don't always stop and reflect on who God is. I don't always look at his creation and marvel at his omnipotence. I don't always stop and drink in his grace or swim in the depths of his mercy. I don't always praise his permanence and immovability. My psalms are often incomplete.

My psalms are anemic and self-centered, and so they really aren't songs of praise worthy to offer God; they aren't really psalms at all. I must praise God if I am ever to complete my songs. Some days this feels impossible. I have to admit that when I am cleaning up cat hairballs and the never-ending pile of dishes in the sink while a toddler screams at me because she is mad that it's Tuesday, I am almost never thinking of how great God is. And when I am overwhelmed with stress from work and housework and just trying to get through the day, I don't usually shout about the amazing work of God around me. I am too focused on shouting down the craziness or shoving chocolate down my throat in a misguided attempt to cope.

But when I get it right, when I sing a whole song to God and really spend time meditating on him, my psalms start to sing out praise and joy. The troubles aren't gone, but they seem infinitely smaller compared to infinite glory and goodness. When I focus on God and his grace, I quit focusing on me, and I am more eager to serve and be kind to people around me. I can see past the pain and frustration at hand and look at the bigger picture. I can know that God is always faithful and unchanging even when my circumstances are difficult. My psalms are complete in those moments. My soul can sing praise even when my eyes are full of tears.

Grief is hard work. Overcoming depression is hard work. It's easy to overlook the eternal joy that knowing God should be when you have forgotten, at least in the face of your pain, what it feels like to be happy. I pray that we can learn how to face what we're feeling, to acknowledge it like this psalmist did, and then to filter it through the truth of who God is to give those feelings perspective and to learn how to live more fully in spite of our losses. So let's start working on that using the Psalm we just read as a guide.

What are you mourning or struggling with? Describe how that makes your body feel and what emotions you feel when you think about your loss. As you name those emotions, write them down or draw them here.

Tell God that you want him to listen to your words. Tell him what you want from him – some action or answer or something you want that only he can provide. Write or draw those things here.

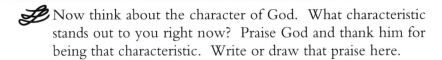 Now think about the character of God. What characteristic stands out to you right now? Praise God and thank him for being that characteristic. Write or draw that praise here.

Even when everything seems to be crumbling around you, you always have something to thank God for in spite of your pain. What good things do you have in your life? What made you smile today? Thank God for those blessings. Write or draw a prayer of thanks here.

When you think of God and the blessings he has given you, does something seem to block you?

Sin separates us from God, and you may need to confess to restore your relationship. Is there some action or words you have spoken that you know were not in line with God's character?

Is there an attitude you are harboring that you need to change and bring in line with the character of God?

If you feel like you don't want to write specifics here, spend some time telling God that you were wrong, and ask him to change your heart. Work on changing your actions or thoughts to keep from repeating that sin. Write or draw that prayer here in as much detail as you feel comfortable. What's on the page matters a whole lot less than being totally honest when you talk to God about it.

Look back at what you wrote or drew that you are struggling with and what you want God to do about it. Now look at what you praised God for. Does what you asked for reflect the character of God, or is it out of line with his goodness?

Think again about what you praised God for. How can you focus on that more often than you focus on your struggling?

A few things work pretty well for me. One is to breathe slowly and repeat, "God is good," as I breathe in. Then I offer him my worry or pain as I breathe out, sometimes even saying, "Take this from me." Another is to write a phrase or a sentence on my hand that will remind me of my reflection on God throughout the day. I write it on my left palm at the base of my thumb so that I will notice the words as I check my watch, which I do a gazillion times a day.

Psychological research pretty squarely links intentional, repeated action to positive mental health change. We know that when we feel sad or angry about our struggling that it's hard to move past it. We have to make a conscious decision to act in a way that realigns our emotions to our beliefs. We need to plan ahead and be ready with a simple act that can draw our focus back to God's goodness and faithfulness.

Make a plan to draw your focus during the day back to what you know to be true of God. This should be a physical action or words that you say out loud throughout the day. Write that plan here.

Chapter 2 – Denial

Denial is the first stage in Elisabeth Kubler-Ross's stages of grief, and it has certainly been the first step in the process for me in each pregnancy loss. I have always thought of myself as a mostly rational being; I'm emotional, sure, but I can see past it to understand facts and logic, so denial seems like an irrational proposition. It is. It is completely irrational to know the truth – I lost my baby – but still find myself thinking, "Oh, I think I just felt him kick!" I knew I was miscarrying, but my brain still processed information and dates based on when the baby would be born. Or I ignored everything and escaped into anything that could hold my interest and keep me from thinking about reality; I learned everything about the Tour de France one summer and continued as an avid cycling fan for a few years. I dove into math once and spent a few months doing algebra equations in my free time.

Denial has taken several forms in my grief journey, but they all boil down to protectionism. My mind was unable to process the data even though my mouth was telling people the facts. I would never have told anyone that I still felt pregnant months after a miscarriage, because it sounds insane – very literally you-need-treatment-crazy. I've seen medical drama plotlines that centered around a crazy woman coming into the E.R. saying she's having a baby, and it turns out she isn't even pregnant. They all ended in psychiatric holds, so I could never admit to anyone that I still felt pregnant sometimes. But still feeling the occasional nausea or leg cramp or fluttery feeling in my gut let me keep moving when everything in my mind wanted to shut down. Telling myself the truth would have been too difficult to bear in those moments. I didn't really believe I was still pregnant, but I also couldn't remind myself I wasn't every moment. There was some levity in the moments that I could forget the miscarriage was happening or had happened.

I will never forget most of the details of my first pregnancy. We had been married for six years when we found out I was pregnant. My husband went with me to the first doctor's appointment, and there was a flurry of congratulations from the nurse, the doctor, and the lab technicians; they gave me a tote bag with the name of the practice printed on it and lots of coupons and baby registry information and free samples. We scheduled my next appointment and headed out into the world flush with our new secret joy. We talked about how to tell our family and friends, and we decided not to wait too long because we're both terrible at keeping secrets. We were going on a vacation to the Bahamas with my husband's family in about a month, so we would need to tell them before we left in case anything happened on the trip. We hit on the perfect plan: Steven's thirtieth birthday was coming up, and we could gather everyone at our house for a surprise birthday party and then turn it around to surprise them when we brought out the cake. We invited all our family and friends, and I ordered a cake that said "Happy Baby" on it with our baby's due date: April 1, 2008. Everyone arrived as planned, my father-in-law was tasked with bringing Steven to his "surprise," and my husband played it off perfectly. No one suspected anything until I set the cake down in front of Steven and he turned it around to face our people and yelled, "Surprise!" instead of blowing out the candles. It was perfect.

Until it wasn't. The next week while we were on vacation, I started spotting. It was very light, but still upsetting; it was our first pregnancy, so anything out of the ordinary was cause for alarm. I called the doctor's office, and they advised me to take it easy and see if that helped it to stop. I slowed my pace, and things settled down. When we had been home for a few days, I decided to try a gentle exercise routine, and in under an hour, I was bleeding. I called the doctor's office again, and they had us come in that day. We didn't talk much while we waited; there was a palpable cloud of worry that hung around us, so words felt strangled and unnecessary.

Finally, we talked to the doctor, and he sent me for an ultrasound. The technician kept asking the same questions about how far along I was and what our expected due date was, but she wouldn't answer any questions, and she didn't point out anything on the monitor. Then we waited for what felt like hours for the doctor to see the scan and then call us back to discuss it. The diagnosis was a blighted ovum, so my baby had stopped developing somewhere around eight weeks (I was eleven weeks along) because there was no fetal pole in the gestational sac, and my body was only just realizing it and beginning to miscarry. I could wait and let things play out naturally, which could take several weeks, or I could have surgery right away.

The thought of waiting for another two weeks was impossible for me to consider, so I opted to have the surgery. It was late Friday afternoon before Labor Day. My doctor and his nurse made every call they could to schedule the procedure for that day, but it was late, and I had eaten lunch, so none of the details would come together. They finally got it set up for the next morning and gave us the check-in instructions. Both our doctor and nurse were compassionate, and they told us to stay in the room for as long as we needed – they could work around us with their other patients, so we didn't need to rush to free up the room. I know that I cried, and I know that my world was cracking apart, but I was mostly numb. I felt like I was watching myself from a distance – like all of those things were happening to me, but in a movie or an alternate universe.

We checked in through the emergency room the next morning, and the pastor of my in-law's church came to be there with Steven's parents and to pray with us before the surgery. He was such a young pastor that Steven and I even joked about him being a kid, but his prayer and presence that morning were comfort and hope in the midst of my bleak fog. I was still watching everything happen to me, and the entire event was surreal. Each nurse and doctor who reviewed my chart and then took me to the next step in the pre-surgery routine would ask me to repeat the name of the procedure I was having. I had several foot surgeries earlier in my life, so I knew it was part of the procedure, but I heard myself over and over tell each medical professional that I was having a d & c (dilation and curettage). Each pronouncement of my baby's death seemed farther and farther removed from my person. Each naming of the procedure was met with a nod that was difficult to read as anything other than approval even though I knew they were just checking off items in the preoperative list. It was all odd. And separate from me. I recall the exact shade of blue of their surgical scrubs, I can probably still draw the face of the nurse who missed five times trying to start my iv, and I can replay the video memory of seeing my doctor's glasses rimmed eyes as he leaned over my face while my vision blurred from the anesthesia. But I see all of it from a perspective outside my body even now, over a decade later.

Denial often feels like numbness in my grief experiences. It may more accurately be described as emotional shock. I wandered through those first days knowing the facts: my baby was dead; I had surgery to complete the miscarriage; we were no longer expecting a child. I thought I was coping pretty well because I wasn't crying very much. I was physically healing well from the surgery. My mouth was saying the things that we all often hear after tragedy like, "It just wasn't God's time," or, "Maybe this is better because there may have been something wrong with the baby if it had kept growing," and, "We can still try again." While all true, these are all imbecilic things to say to someone who just had a miscarriage — especially if that person is yourself — but I didn't know that yet. The fact that I could repeat them and say them to family and friends, and especially myself, tells me now just how much I had failed to process at that point.

I wasn't feeling much pain; I wasn't feeling much of anything because my emotions had basically shut down. I was subconsciously ignoring my feelings, which isn't a good thing to do for long, but in the short term it allowed me time to deal with the physical recovery.

In subsequent miscarriages, I experienced that same numbness and fog; while I didn't tell myself any of the original platitudes, I would explain to loved ones that I would be numb for a few days or weeks, and then I would be forgetful for the next several months, and then I would work through anger and depression. But I also experienced straight up denial; I let myself believe that all of the lab work would be great even when I knew my body was already miscarrying. I would look in the mirror and pretend that I had a pregnant belly. I would dream about my lost babies, and I would wake up believing that it had just been a nightmare, and I didn't really lose each and every pregnancy. Oh, how I could deny. The denial of actual facts never lasted long except in my dreams, but I denied that I was hurt. I denied that my soul was untethered and that I was struggling to actually face my pain.

I was an expert in avoiding my pain, but most of my methods were really destructive. I ate a lot, and I shopped a lot, and I threw myself into volunteering and starting a lot of craft projects (though only a few got finished...). That avoidance is denial, but after the initial shock of loss has helped you walk through the early days of grief more or less on autopilot, it's time to start facing the loss and stepping out of denial.

Denial has its place. Facing the enormity of your loss all at once is impossible; it is a process. You can't experience a loss and just be fine in a few minutes. You won't be fine for a while, but there may be things that you have to do to keep living and deal with the loss at hand. In the case of a lost loved one, you may have to prepare a funeral; when you lose a job, you have to clear your workspace and actually exit the building. You still have to feed yourself, and you may have people depending on you to take care of them. You still have to function at some level even in the face of deep hurt and loss. Enter denial. As a short-term process it will short-circuit some of the overwhelming feelings, which will allow you to move through the initial experience of loss. You can't live there. I tried. It's not healthy. But don't feel alone or afraid if you find yourself experiencing denial as you face your grief.

Let's look at how some of the Psalms deal with denial. We'll work through several psalms to see examples of how our psalmist guides expressed their denial to God, and we'll start putting this stage of the journey into perspective in order to work through it. Read Psalm 101 and Psalm 81.

Psalm 101

Psalm 101 is not on its face a psalm of denial; it is a model for life and leadership, and it is likely an oath David made to God to live out his faith. It is a model of perfect faith in practice, and when I read it I saw both the hope and promise of David's heart and my own attempts to live perfectly and to gloss over my pain by denying it was affecting me. Of course we can't live perfectly all the time. If it were as easy as outlining the steps, as David does here, and then following them unerringly, we wouldn't need Jesus.

I am an excellent planner. I can't even tell you how many times I have laid out an exercise and diet plan and charted my expected weight loss down to the pound until I met my goal weight – or how many times I have plotted the perfect schedule that would allow me time to work, write, clean house, and play with my daughter every day.

My plans are all perfect, but they are mostly rooted in denial. I forget that I can't work my way to perfection by following an airtight schedule. I ignore that the reason I need to lose weight is because I overeat when I am stressed or when I feel uncomfortable emotions, and so I leave the reason for the plan unaddressed. I swear, just like David, that I will live excellently for God, but I forget to start with God when I make my plans. If I started by talking to God first, I would see that I need to show him my problems first, and then listen for his guidance before I assume I can follow through on my well-intentioned but still Anne-breathed checklist for perfect living. No matter how hopeful I am at the beginning, I am doomed to fail.

What about David and this psalm? Did he live out his life perfectly from this oath forward? Not quite. David has always been called a "man after God's own heart" and praised for his strong faith that allowed him to conquer Goliath, to outlive Saul's attempts to kill him, and to become a triumphant king of Israel. But along the way, he lied, he committed adultery and murder, and he made some bad calls as a leader. In the moment he wrote Psalm 101, David was full of hope and promise and love for God, but he was essentially in denial that he was human.

Don't we all do this? We do it in the face of loss, and we do it in the face of our imperfection. Grief is the result of imperfection; it is the loss of some perfect condition. Biblically speaking, perfect means whole or complete, so loss makes us instantaneously incomplete, imperfect. We react with denial to project that we are still whole and perfect to the world, both to avoid our feelings and to hide our perceived weakness. So we lose our focus on our relationship with God, build a perfect plan, and swear to be better and stronger. We may even be planning some great work for God, but we aren't really following God when we set out to be perfect by checking everything off the to-do list. Maybe this is the most insidious form of denial because on the surface it looks like faith.

I have no idea if David was in denial when he wrote this, but by only stating his promise in terms of perfection David reflects my own tendencies when I am in the midst of denial. We don't know what particular circumstances led to David penning this promise, so maybe he had already faced his demons and was entering this plan with God as his guide. We know he failed when he took his eyes off of God and placed his faith in himself. We also know he returned to God after every mistake and that David sought God in the midst of every loss and pain he faced. So even if he vowed to be perfect in a moment of denial, David still offers us a model of how to handle loss by pouring our hearts out to God and trusting him to lift up our eyes and provide us tools to walk through it.

What does denial look like in your life? Have you ever tried to perfect plan your way out of the heavy emotions of loss? Take some space to look at how you can confront denial with God and what it's like when you try to do it without him.

Psalm 81

When we read Psalm 81, denial is probably not the first thing that comes to mind. This psalm was written by Asaph as a song to call Israel to praise and to stay true to their one and only God. What strikes me in this psalm is that it offers a path out of denial and into the light of truth. God points out their denial, and he shows them the consequences of continuing on that path. In the first three verses, Asaph's psalm calls the people of Israel together to praise God. The New Moon feast day was an established celebration for the people of Israel to worship together – like a Sunday morning worship service but a little bigger. The two most important things to take away from this section of Psalm 81 in reference to grief are that we are *always* called to worship God, and we are most effective at putting that into practice when we do it as a group.

Asaph is calling his people to encourage one another to praise by adding to the collective noise of worship. Look at how each bit of music referenced crescendos to the trumpet sound: sing, shout, play instruments, blow the trumpet. It's hard to raise that kind of ruckus by yourself. While praising Jesus as a body of believers is important for our worship, it also strengthens our relationship bonds outside of our corporate worship experience. Having strong ties to other people is key to effectively coping with grief and depression. You can't do it all alone.

Consider your relationships and your current experience of worship. Do you praise God with other believers often? If not, pray for God to show you a safe place to go and praise him with a body of Christ.

When you experience corporate worship, do you find that your heart is more open to those around you? Shared experiences enable us to build relationships on that common ground, which is amplified in the body of Christ because we also share core beliefs that provide a deeper foundation to build on.

Draw or write ways that this foundation and strong relationships can help you cope with your loss.

Verses 4–10 provide the basis for our trust in God. He established feast days for Israel to serve as a testimony to the rest of the world of his provision for them and as a reminder to the Israelites that he alone was the source of their salvation: "You called in trouble, and I delivered you." God's established rule provides a safe framework for us live in; we can test our emotions against his truth and reveal the destructive feelings we so often want to act on.

What happens when you hold your emotions and the thoughts they provoke up to the light of God's established truth? I most often discover that I am letting pain whisper lies to my soul that God doesn't love me, and he doesn't want the best for me, or I wouldn't be feeling this pain. Without his truth, I am tempted to believe it and sink further into depression, denying my pain by numbing it with food or watching too much television. But every time I take a moment to really examine what I'm feeling and then compare it to what I know of God's character, I see that he is always true and unchanging and good. My circumstances may be beyond awful, but God is always good, and I can always trust him.

What feelings are you denying right now?

What are you avoiding holding up to the light of God's brilliantly shining truth?

Think of his established rule as a prism that sorts each emotion we have into its purest form so that we can understand the depths of what we are feeling.

Take some time to dwell on your denial, and then list or sketch out each feeling like a ray of color refracted through the prism. Once you sort out the emotions and where they are coming from inside you, think of them from the perspective of God's character. Does your anger hold up to God's light? Does your fear have a basis in his love? For each emotion you named, tell it the truth that you see reflected in God's character.

God doesn't want us to remain in the mess we're in. He always calls us higher and closer to him, and we see that in verses 11-16. Israel denied God, so he left them to their own devices. Historically, the Israelites followed a cycle of obeying God, forgetting that God was the reason they were successful, disobeying God, getting wiped out by enemy forces, and then coming back to God for help. At every point in God's relationship with Israel, he offers them the choice of following him in truth and enjoying his protection or following their own desires apart from him and living with the destruction that inevitably brings. In terms of denial at this stage in grief, you are faced with a choice just like the Israelites. You can face your pain with God's truth and work through it, or you can stay where you are in self-destructive coping mechanisms that are only masking your pain or numbing it for brief amounts of time.

Can you afford to stay where you are in denial?

Look down the road at what the end result of your current denial behaviors will be if left unchecked. Now look at God's promises to Israel if they would listen and follow him (Psalm 81:14-16). God can take out your enemies (that pain and fear and anger...). He will feed your soul and satisfy you if you will let him.

What will it take for you to allow God to show you his truth and for you to follow him? Draw or write out those reflections.

Chapter 3 – Anger

Anger is the easiest emotion in loss for me to both feel and identify. If I am brutally honest, anger is, at least temporarily, a pretty satisfying emotion: I feel righteous and somehow vindicated; it's a powerful energy, even though it's hugely destructive. Anger is an easy go-to as a default emotion or as a first emotion post-denial because it's simple to be mad. All I have to do is look around me, and I can find some injustice to trigger my wrath – terrible customer service, my dog shredding trash all over the kitchen, my daughter's inexplicable need to cover nine tenths of the floor with glitter glue and sequins, pregnant bellies in every aisle of the grocery store... And then I hit on the real reason I'm angry at the world: I'm angry with God and the circumstances he put me in.

I grew up attending church regularly, and I went to a Baptist college, so I have heard a lot of people perform linguistic and theological contortions to explain why bad things happen. Read Job. His friends say most of the things "church people" say about why bad things happen to good people. One of my least favorite theological contortion acts involves God's "active will" and his "permissive will." The basic idea is that God's active will involves things he directly does or enacts in order to bring a certain thing to pass; his permissive will involves all the things that he doesn't directly enact but rather allows to happen. I have trouble marrying these two ideas for two reasons – God is omnipotent, omniscient, and omnipresent, so passivity seems to be a contradiction; and choosing not to act is itself an act, so passive versus active seems to be a silly idea to make us feel better about reality. The reality is that we live in a world broken by sin where terrible things will happen because we cannot humanly achieve perfection. A perfect world will never exist until God creates his new heaven and new earth, so until then evil can and will run rampant.

To continue the brutally honest streak, I have spent a lot of time furious with God. I was a little angry about losing our first baby, and I was moderately angry after my second miscarriage, but by the fifth, I quit moving on to other stages of grief. I lived in anger. I remember going to a grief support group after our second miscarriage, and all of the other people had lost adult or teenage children. They each had a cause of death for their loved one — a crash or a disease or a person they could blame — a direction in which to channel their anger, something to point at and crusade against. As twisted as it was emotionally, I was jealous of them and their targets; I had no diagnosis, and there was no one to blame except for God and his "passive will."

Maybe God didn't actively kill my babies, but he could have stopped them from dying. Legally, there's a distinction between perpetrating a crime and failing to prevent a crime, but they're both awful acts that result in crime. So I blamed God. I yelled at him, and I cussed at him in terms middle school boys would envy and sailors would blush to hear. I let him have it, and then I pouted and refused to listen to him or speak to him. I took every pregnancy and birth announcement as a personal insult from him; every song of worship, every earnest prayer I heard at church felt like salt rubbing in my open wounds. God was surely not good, and I could not even sing a hymn because my heart was so broken and bitter. I just sat through church waiting for it to be over.

My anger quickly boiled over into every aspect of my life, and it is still the hardest thing to face and eradicate in my life. Anger itself isn't a problem; it's usually a symptom of something broken in our minds and hearts. Anger is a problem when we act from that emotion and when we feed that feeling and continue to live with it rather than acknowledge it and look deeper. How can we feel anger without acting on it?

First, allow yourself to express the anger without feeling guilty that you are experiencing that emotion. Tell God exactly how you feel, and don't hold back – he already knows what's in your heart and in your head, so you're not going to surprise him – and then allow that expression to help you look deeper past the anger to what it masks.

Next, examine the anger and what triggers it. Never stop at merely expressing anger; let that be a cue to examine its origin and work through it. What do the triggers tell you about the root of your anger? What specific pain is that anger masking?

I found that I was angry at myself and my body for betraying me and losing my babies, and I was furious that I had lost the beauty and wonder and joy of pregnancy. That was a pulsating, raw pain that ripped open and gaped more and more with each loss, and it took years of distance to even scab over. Beyond that, I was angry with God for allowing my circumstances to be other than what I had imagined for my journey into parenthood. Admitting (even to myself) that I was angry with God was one of the most difficult things I've ever done in my faith walk, but it was also freeing, as if the confession of my rage cleared the air and purged the sharpest parts of it from my soul.

God knows when we're angry; he knows what's causing the emotion, and he knows what the underlying pain is that makes our anger burn so hotly. It's no surprise to him that you may feel this way. It's not a sin to feel angry. The sin comes in when we act out of our anger and cause harm and do things we know aren't right but excuse them anyway because we are angry. We may discuss the difference between righteous anger and regular anger, but the bottom line is: we can feel angry for a time, but we can't live there. We definitely can't base our actions on it.

Like denial, anger has its place. It can fuel us and keep us moving in moments when we have accepted our new reality, but it's just too much to bear. It's a simple emotion to feel. After dealing with the details immediately surrounding a loss, like arrangements or moving or searching for a job, we can be left completely emotionally exhausted – too tired to deal with the other complex emotions that are breaking through our denial defense systems. Anger is simple. Anger is easy to come by. But anger has to be a stage that we pass through, and we must beware the damage we can cause to everyone around us if we indulge in acting out our anger in destructive ways.

I once took up kickboxing classes because that would be a "legal" way to punch the crap out of something. It was productive on two fronts: I was venting my rage on an inanimate object, and I was exercising my body. In comparison, yelling at my child like a raving lunatic because I lose my temper too easily when I'm feeling depression or grief symptoms only causes harm to our relationship. We must evaluate our expressions of anger and choose wisely when is an appropriate to let them run amok.

There are plenty of examples of anger in the Psalms, so let's examine the psalmist's approach to expressing and resolving anger. We'll be reading through Psalms 39, 44, and 52.

Psalm 44

Let's start with Psalm 44. The opening verses sound nothing like anger. They list things that God has done for the nation of Israel, and verse 8 ends this first song verse with a promise to praise God forever. But then verse 9 happens. What follows is a list of things God did to hurt Israel: you cast us off, you made us retreat, you sell your people, you make us a reproach and a byword. That's a giant shift from the first list of God's accomplishments. As a writer of poems, I admire the contrast, but as a reader, I feel a little confused by the sudden change in tone, at least until I considered it in terms of grief. Your emotions can turn on a dime in times of loss, and that is clearly what this psalmist was experiencing. They had gone from victory under God's leadership to ugly defeat, and our psalmist was obviously struggling to come to terms with the sudden loss. He was angry with God for abandoning his people.

Have you ever been surprised by how quickly your emotions can spin out from happily praising God to making a bullet point list of all the ways he's done you wrong? Maybe you haven't experienced this in your relationship with God, but I bet you've done it with people around you. Life with your friend or spouse or coworker is just fine until you suddenly have a million reasons to kick them in the shins.

Take a moment to examine the times in your relationships that have been interrupted by a sudden onset of rage.

Was there a specific trigger?

Were you able to hold your tongue and stop from listing your grievances?

When you lose your temper quickly and somewhat unexpectedly, what do you think is happening to the people around you and your relationships with them?

As you think about those questions, write or draw out the relationships that have been affected by your anger.

We'll continue this line of thought a little further, but now that you have an idea what damage your anger has caused, let's take some time to think about how to handle it instead. You can express your outrage directly, as our psalmist did, but that has some direct and often harmful side effects. We need to find a better way to vent without hurting anyone.

One way to do this is to write all of your angry outburst in a journal or a letter that you never intend to send. I've done this quite a bit. If you don't want to keep a written reminder of how you felt, especially once you realize that it was a temporary emotion in the face of a much deeper pain, think about a symbolic way to destroy the pages. Once you've purged the anger in a way that won't harm anyone, and it allowed you to vent rather than boil over, maybe burn the pages. Let them go in a way that they can never come back into your heart, and release them permanently. If writing isn't your thing, draw out your feelings. Let your pen or paints reflect the jagged edges that hurt so badly, and pour the emotions onto the page to release them. Find a way to let your anger escape safely without harming the relationships that you so desperately need to carry you through this time of grief. Make a plan now for how you will handle your anger the next time it threatens to take over. Write it down and practice putting every angry thought – no matter how slight – through this process. The more you practice when it's not a big deal, the more likely you are to handle it well when it is a big deal.

As we continue in Psalm 44, in verses 17 through 22 our psalmist points back at God and says, "You did all this to us, but we never forgot you or failed to follow you." I don't know about you, but when I'm very honest with myself, this is how I feel about my pregnancy losses. I've been faithful to God – I've been a good person my whole life – but God let this thing happen to me. (It looks like our psalmist doesn't care about God's "passive will" either...)

We just spent time thinking about what anger does in our relationships with other humans. It can drive us away

46

from God, too. We're conditioned to think that being angry with God is a sin, so we can never admit that we feel that way to ourselves or anyone else.

The problem is that we're being dishonest with God when we don't tell him how we're really feeling. Do you really think the God who created every cell in your body doesn't know what you're thinking? Do you really think ignoring the proverbial elephant in the room is going to make your anger go away? It doesn't work in our human relationships, and it's not going to work with God. Maybe we in the modern church are afraid to be disrespectful of our heavenly Father by being mad, but here's an example of doing just that *in the Bible.* (Jonah is also a great example of this.) Jesus told us to bring him our burdens and trade them for his grace, so give God your anger and let him transform it. I promise that being honest in your prayer will change it radically for the better.

What anger are you harboring towards God? Even if you're afraid to, express it to him right now. As you pray and reflect (don't be surprised if God starts to show you truths that will curb your anger), open your heart wide open to your creator.

Write or draw how it feels to be honest with God.

Our psalmist isn't done yet. Verses 23 through 26 are a call for God to get up and do something to save his people, and he's not afraid to tell God exactly what he wants him to do and why. Let me be very clear right here that we will not get everything that we ask God for, no matter how earnestly we pray for it. What we will get is exactly what we need to glorify God where we are and to fulfill his purpose for us.

Verse 26 sets the example for how to pray this way. "Rise up! Help us! Ransom us because of your unfailing love." (Psalms 44:26 NLT)

What do you need from God to survive this moment?

How can you glorify him in your circumstances right now, and what can he do to redeem you for his mercies' sake?

Continue to be honest and pray right now for him to rise up and help you.

Write your own psalm here about what God has done in your life to provide for you, how your loss has changed you, and what your life will be like when you see God step in and redeem you.

Psalm 52

Psalm 52 was written by David while he was at war with Saul, and Saul was actively trying to kill him, even though David was best friends with Saul's son and married to one of Saul's daughters. He suddenly found himself in the crosshairs of a king who knew that God wanted Saul off the throne and David on it. David was on defense against Saul while still protecting his country from armed invaders. That's a pretty tough gig. I imagine he felt attacked from every side. It would be completely understandable to find David angry, especially at Saul, and that's what we see in the first seven verses here. He describes Saul's pride and duplicity, and then he tells how God will destroy him.

We'd probably classify this as "righteous anger." David has obvious reason to rage against the evils of Saul, and he's accurate about Saul's character. I think there's no questioning of David's motives in pronouncing God's judgment on Saul's unrepentant actions, but I saw myself and my human desire to compare myself to others who are openly sinning when I read this Psalm. It is so tempting to look at the circumstances of our loss and then look at the world full of horrible people who seem to be prospering. I can't even tell you how many times I told God how unfair it was that I lost baby after baby while I watched women on drugs deliver babies addicted to horrible substances and read seemingly endless news stories about children being abused. How could God give these wretched people children while I lost every child I carried?

Anger can twist our perspective so that even what may be considered righteous anger is something unholy and selfish. David avoided that trap by placing his trust and his focus where it belonged. The last two verses of Psalm 52 express David's commitment to God and what his life will be like in comparison to Saul's inevitable doom. History tells us that David's patience in the face of his anger was rewarded in his relationship with God as well as materially. When we praise Jesus and place him at the center of our focus rather than ourselves, we will be able to control our anger and see it in perspective.

What do you do when you compare your situation to someone else and feel anger at how unfair your circumstances feel?

How can you actively focus on the rewards of maintaining a strong relationship in faith to God?

Brainstorm at least three ways you can redirect your angry thoughts to the truth of living in God's mercy.

Psalm 39

Psalm 39 offers more insight into productively expressing anger and how to turn to God for help in healing it. In the opening of this psalm, David notes that the wickedness around him is making him burn hot with anger, but he determines to keep his mouth shut to avoid speaking foolishly in his anger.

He gave the situation some space.

Look closely at verse 2. He doesn't say anything at all in the moment, not even something good, because he knows he may not be able to control his tongue if he sets it loose. When he does speak, he prays and asks God to remind him how fleeting his life is so that he will keep his hope in what is infinite and steadfast rather than fleeting.

What would your anger look like if you could press mute on it and consider what that moment looks like compared to your whole lifespan?

Now compare it to eternity. If we are a quickly passing fog in the midst of the universe, our hope in Christ is the only thing that will last.

Now look closely at verse 9. David knows that his mute button wasn't controlled by him but by God. We can't hold back rage without some divine intervention; it's a powerful feeling that too easily escapes control, but it's possible the more we hand control over to God. This doesn't just make David a better person. It also quiets his mind enough to process the real anguish he was feeling and pour that out to his creator as well. Once the anger is silent, he can hear and feel the root cause of the pain. He doesn't end this psalm on a high note of praise, but he continues to be honest with God about his broken heart.

Give some space to your anger and let God help you push the mute button.

What do you see underneath the anger that's causing your pain?

 Take some time to write or draw that out and tell your creator what's in your heart.

A side note on anger: irritability is a symptom of depression. If you find yourself losing it over everything for an extended period of time (let's say a month), you need to have your mental health evaluated. It is completely normal to suffer some episodic depression after a loss, but if it persists for more than a few months, or you have thoughts of harming yourself or others, please go to your doctor or to a therapist – or both!

You deserve good mental health, but you can't heal well from grief if you are also experiencing lingering clinical depression. Very often, you will notice that you feel down, but anger is often as prominent a symptom as sadness. I put off going to therapy because I wasn't feeling very sad all the time. I was cranky all the time and overwhelmed by everything, and I was clinically depressed. For me, medication and talk therapy were the way out. I'm healthy enough now to have stopped the medication, but I still have to stay on top of good self-care habits and the occasional therapy session. Depression will be a lifelong battle for me. It may not be for you, but don't neglect your mental and emotional health.

If you can't afford a therapist, seek out a pastor for help. If they can't counsel you, they will help you find someone who is equipped and will work within your budget. If going to a church scares you, start with your doctor; they will help you find appropriate care. I wholeheartedly believe that God can supernaturally heal us physically, mentally, emotionally, spiritually, but I also know that most healing is done through the tools he equips us with. If journaling and prayer aren't helping, you need to expand your toolbox. It doesn't mean your faith is weak to seek help outside the church. It means your faith is strong enough to see that God may be asking you to trust him past the walls of the church. If you will go to the doctor when you are sick, seeking mental health assistance is no different.

Chapter 4 – Bargaining

I've made a lot of bargains with God in my lifetime, usually silly, like, "If you'll help me with this test, then I promise not to put off studying again." People for all of recorded history have offered extreme sacrifices or pilgrimages if God will just do what they ask. Bargaining is almost always an attempt to game the system or to avoid the real consequences of our actions (or lack thereof in the case of my study habits). It's a way to try to maintain a semblance of control over our circumstances. In grief, it's roughly the same thing. Maybe we're not responsible for the loss, but we are trying to avoid the consequences of it by offering something to God in trade.

Most of my attempted deals with God involved the duration of my own suffering or the safety of other people's pregnancies. As soon as I knew about each pregnancy, I began praying for God to either end it quickly and decisively or to let this be the one pregnancy that went to term. God only answered that request the way I wanted him to once. The other ten pregnancies ended badly, and most of them dragged on for weeks – several of them even for months. When it became obvious that my negotiations weren't working the way I wanted on my own behalf, I started telling God that my suffering ought to take the place of someone else's pain. My pregnancy losses should substitute for my friend's, so she wouldn't have to experience such devastation. This tactic failed, too. I was furious to learn that a friend of mine lost a baby late in her pregnancy, and God hadn't honored my deal.

Of course, the problem with negotiating with God is that we humans hold none of the cards, and God has them all. He not only holds all the cards but he also runs the table; he doesn't need our counsel to operate the universe. I made deals with God, but I hadn't bothered to find out if God agreed to my terms. And they were all my terms. I also hadn't bothered to consult God on what he wanted in my situation. Bargaining is pointless if you have nothing to offer the other party. As a human, I have nothing to offer God that didn't come from him to begin with.

As a coping mechanism, bargaining was a way of coming to terms with the reality of the situation while still clinging to hope that it could change if I could just offer God the right sacrifice, the right action, or the right prayer. My bargains helped me begin to process the loss, even when I wasn't ready to accept yet another miscarriage as my fate. Negotiating gave me the illusion that I could control something that was spinning wildly beyond my control.

I have had very few instances in my life when I heard the voice of God speak clear, direct words to me. I have heard him speak to me through the Bible or through experiences, but for me it is rare to hear more than nudges or realizations that clarify what I know of God or what he wants me to do. One night I had been praying and crying to God to comfort me, to let me physically feel him hold me and comfort me like a child. I begged him to just let me never get pregnant again if I was only ever going to lose babies (another failed bargaining attempt), or to just let me know beyond the shadow of a doubt that we should stop trying to get pregnant. He didn't directly answer either request, but very clearly he told me, "I can give you what you want now, or you can keep waiting, and I'll give you what's in my plan for you. Taking what you want right now may feel better for a while, but it's not the best thing." I heard those words like he said them out loud sitting right next to me, and then the only thing I could think of was Jeremiah 29:11, *"For I know the plans I have for you,' says the Lord. 'They are plans for good and not for disaster, to give you a future and a hope.'" NLT*

God counter-offered. Just one time, my bargaining included the other party in the negotiations, and God made a very clear offer. I could accept a quick ending to this particular suffering, which wasn't the best plan that God already had written for me, or I could wait and continue to endure until he dazzled us. I chose to wait. I decided that if it was important enough for God to speak so directly to me then it was important enough to wait and see what he had planned. I'd like to say that ended my negotiating, but I still find myself offering God plea deals when I'm faced with overwhelming stress.

I was glad to find that the psalmists weren't immune to this all-too-human coping strategy. Let's look at how David and others bargained with God. Let's read Psalms 7, 10, 31, 54, and 61.

Psalm 7

In Psalm 7, we find David crying out to God to protect him and to stand up against his enemies. Often in negotiating, we use the consequences of inaction as a bargaining chip, especially when we're talking to God. David is a perfect example of this: *"I come to you for protection, O Lord my God. Save me from my persecutors – rescue me! If you don't, they will maul me like a lion, tearing me to pieces with no one to rescue me."* (Psalms 7:1-2 NLT) David wastes no time jumping right in with his request for rescue and telling God what the consequences will be if he doesn't step in. He follows this by telling God that he welcomes destruction if he has actually committed a wrong or injustice before he asks God to *"Arise, O Lord, in anger! Stand up against the fury of my enemies! Wake up, my God, and bring justice!"* (Psalms 7:6 NLT)

This sounds like bargaining with a splash of anger, doesn't it? But what's important to see here is that not even David was immune from the desire for self-preservation. He believed that he had more to do in his life, and he was sure that continuing to live would glorify God. Even though David was convinced of his innocence, he still gave room for God to wipe him out instead of his enemy if David was actually the offending party. David bargained with God for his life because it would bring glory to God; David also acknowledged God as the judge and authority over all life and asked God to judge between him and his enemy by rescuing David.

Our circumstances are not often life or death like David's in this psalm. What we have in common with David's bargaining with God is we're trying to trade the awfulness of our reality for something that we think will be less awful (or even a miracle) because we think that will glorify God. We're not wrong to ask God to preserve us or to work a miracle, but we must be willing to accept that what we ask may not always be the circumstances that God will bring about. What we ask may not be the glory God wants to achieve through us. His plans are always bigger than we imagine, and they always show us that God is holy and worthy of his throne.

In the bargaining stage of grief, we are acknowledging our reality, but we're not ready to accept it as it is. What we can do differently as Christ followers is to filter our bargaining through the lens of glorifying God. Even if you make God an offer to glorify him by giving you exactly what you asked for, are you willing to glorify him now in the midst of your loss as well as in the future, regardless of what he does to answer your prayer?

We see that in Psalm 7, even though we also see the rawness of David's fear and pain. David was willing to love and follow and give God the glory in every circumstance, no matter how God answered his prayers.

What bargains have you made with God?
Describe them here in words or pictures.

Psalm 10

Psalm 10 echoes the tone of David's Psalm 7 by pointing out the evil around him and begging God to take it away. In my own life, this has probably been the most common form of bargaining I do — just begging God to take away the hurt and everything that comes with it. I have asked, just like this psalmist, "Where are you God? Don't you see what's happening here? Why aren't you fixing this?" Psalm 10 is focused on asking God to heal the land of wickedness and injustice.

Read this psalm again, but substitute your loss for the sections about the wicked. Does this sound like something you've prayed?

How does it feel to earnestly beg God to change your situation?

Do you believe that he can?

Take some time to rewrite Psalm 10 in your own words with your particular circumstances included.

Psalm 31

Psalm 31 is another work of David begging God to help him in his distress. This one stands out to me because of his description of his grief in verses 9 through 13. It also stands out because of his declaration in verse 14: *"But I am trusting you, O Lord, saying, 'You are my God!'" (NLT)* David has already asked God to save him for the sake of God's reputation as good and faithful, and he has told God just how horrible his grief is. Now David is adding, "I trust you no matter what because you are my God." Just like now, there were options in David's time for who to worship. There were household gods that people worshipped for fertility, harvests, wealth, beauty... He could have put his trust in himself, his abilities, his intuition; or he could have found comfort in objects like food, wealth, and sex.

Just like today, there were a million different things David could have turned to as a way to comfort his pain. But David reiterated his trust in God, even when he was dying on the inside from his grief. He declared, *"My future is in your hands." (Psalms 31:15a NLT)* David knew that whatever God chose for his future would be good because he had already witnessed God's provision for him in the past. He knew that God would always bestow his lovingkindness on those who love the Lord.

Read the psalm you wrote earlier. You've already answered whether or not you believe God can do what you ask, but now ask yourself if you trust God no matter whether he answers your prayer exactly the way you asked or not.

Do you trust him to guard your heart and to bring about glory for his name through your grief?

Reflect on that question for a few minutes and note what comes to mind.

Psalms 54 and 61

When we look at Psalms 54 and 61, they have very similar themes. They both ask for God to rescue David so that David can serve him longer on earth – Psalm 61 promises that he will sing God's praises forever. David's bargaining seems to be, "I'm no good to you dead, so rescue me, and I'll praise you louder and be a good king for you." What's a little different than some of the other psalms we've looked at is that both of these focus a lot more on the goodness of God beyond immediate rescue from enemies.

We get the idea in both of these psalms that David has already been rescued and is making good on his earlier bargains with God. David was seeking the preservation of his life, which we know happened. What we don't know is how the details of what actually transpired compared to what David asked of God. It's a pretty safe bet that God didn't do everything the way David planned, just like God probably won't bring us through our pain exactly the way we imagined he would. Even though there were surely things David didn't want to accept about his circumstances, he still trusted and praised God for saving him.

Are you willing to be used in the midst of your loss to bring glory to God?

What do you think that looks like in your life right now?

Are you willing to trust God even when your circumstances aren't exactly what you bargained for?

Chapter 5 – Depression

Depression is a hard stage of grief to get a hold of because it's so difficult to identify. I think we struggle to name our emotions simply and without spin. If someone asks how we're doing, we tend to answer that we are "fine," or that we feel a little sad, but we're getting better every day. We want to qualify the emotion when it's negative, maybe to "fake it 'til we make it" and convince ourselves that we're okay, maybe to make someone else feel more comfortable with our grief, or maybe to hide the fact that we're not coping so well. I believe we do ourselves and everyone who loves us a disservice by hiding our sadness.

We aren't built to walk through life alone; God designed us for the richness of community – to be the Body of Christ. We can't heal completely if we try it alone, and we don't allow the body to function as it should if we don't allow ourselves to be taken care of when we need it. God didn't design us to only serve others and never rely on anyone but ourselves when we need help. Our culture celebrates pulling yourself up by the bootstraps and moving on, and it doesn't value vulnerability and weakness. But God does. He honors our weakness by making it a way to show his strength through us. When we let other people in when we're struggling with sadness and depression, God mobilizes the Body of Christ and puts his people to use. If you're willing to be used by God, then you must be willing to be served by his people, too.

If you're like me, you have no trouble caring for other people, but just stating simply, "I'm sad," and letting someone sit with you through a sad spell is intensely difficult. It's hard to let go of being in control and to let someone step in to help. It's hard to be vulnerable and share the parts of you that aren't social media worthy. It's hard to hurt. I know I'd like to skip pain as often as possible. I don't want to be sad because it's painful and miserable. I don't cry pretty, either. I am a snuffling, snotty, puffy-faced mess of a crier, and it's hard to stop once I start. The thing is, though, loss hurts us very deeply, and we will have to deal with that pain as part of the healing process. Much as I hate the ugly cry, it's necessary to express our sadness if we are to move on from it.

Depression is an inevitable stage of grief, and it's something that I still deal with on and off – and probably will for the rest of my life. As part of grief, depression should be a short-term stage, but if you find yourself thinking about harming yourself or others, if you can't function in your daily routines even several weeks after your loss, or if you can't move past the depression after what seems like a reasonable amount of time to you, please seek professional help. It's good to let your friends and family in to help you, but understand that there is only so much they can do. Your average friend is not a professionally trained therapist; even if they were, you need your friends to be friends and not professionals in your life. Therapists can work with you through incredibly hard and intensely personal situations, and sometimes that professional distance allows you to open up in ways you won't with a friend or family member. And you can talk to them without fear of repercussions in your friendship. The bottom line is, if you find yourself stuck in the same place for too long, take a hard look at what kind of help you need to get past it.

In my life, depression tends to manifest itself as irritability and a complete lack of motivation about everything; everything – emotions, sensory inputs, work tasks, housekeeping – is overwhelming. I know I need to get up in the morning to start the day, but I am filled with dread about everything the day offers, and I just keep hitting "snooze" on the alarm. When I finally convince myself that I must move, it is a herculean effort to get out of bed, and every physical task is draining, like I am moving through knee-deep sand with every step. It feels like nothing will go right, and every circumstance is engineered to magnify how badly the day will go. I can't even make myself do things that I know would make me feel better, like exercise, writing, or painting. I feel like I am less than a slug. I believe the lies swirling through my thoughts, and I believe that my emotions are the truth. I forget (or, more accurately, ignore) God. I don't listen to what he says about who I am.

So how do you move past a seemingly insurmountable emotional state? In the case of mild depression, start slowly, and change one thing at a time. Make yourself go for a walk every day. Spend time every day reading the Bible and praying. Then spend some time participating in hobbies that you love. Tell yourself several times a day that you are a dearly loved, wonderfully made child of God. It will feel impossible, but you can do hard things. God promises to give us strength to do all things that glorify him (Philippians 4:13), and you are no exception to this promise. If you need to, set a timer, start with as little as five minutes, and add a minute each day until you find you are able to function more freely and more joyfully. It takes time to break through the fog, but each time that you do, more and more light will come in. Eventually there will be more light than fog, and you will see life clearly enough to realize that the depression is fading, and the overwhelm and sluggishness will dissipate as the light takes over.

More severe depression will not lift so easily. I am a huge fan of therapy, and it helps to have an outside, expert opinion on how you're coping. Therapists can help you develop coping skills, and they can help you filter your emotions and see past them to the truth. As much as we want to believe them, our emotions are not the truth. Talk therapy is a wonderful tool to alleviate depression, but sometimes even therapy isn't enough to cut through the fog. I needed medication to begin to make progress. The antidepressant didn't make the depression go away, but it alleviated enough of the symptoms that I could start to manage it with healthy coping tools. There are no instant fixes; there are lots of tools for you to learn, and there is lots of hard work involved in learning how to use them. The tough truth is that no one can take that first step to ask for help for you, and no one can do the work for you. But you can do hard things, and you can get healthier and stronger.

I have not been depressed for great lengths of time in the last few years, but I still deal with bouts that will last for days or weeks. Maybe the greatest coping tool for me is the ability to recognize the symptoms and begin to counter them as soon as I recognize that depression is creeping back in. I call it "depression brain," and I am determined not to let depression brain win. I have to keep working on my mental health by doing things every day that I know will help me be more resilient and more able to feel emotions and move on without letting them control me. It's not always easy. When I'm not in regular therapy sessions, I use journaling to express my feelings and think about what's behind them so I can address the root of depression brain. I also read books and listen to podcasts that teach me more about good coping tools to add to my arsenal. I doubt that the process of learning and working through depression brain symptoms will ever end. I've learned that when I skip out on this work for weeks or months at a time, I fall harder and further into depression brain mode when it flares back up.

I have met with no shame or disappointment from my family or my church about dealing with depression or needing medication, but I think that the church as a whole tends to ignore depression as an issue beyond spirituality. We have miles to go on this issue – very often we are like the example Jesus gave of how *not* to handle people in real physical need: *"Suppose you see a brother or sister who has no food or clothing, and you say, 'Good-bye and have a good day; stay warm and eat well' – but then you don't give that person any food or clothing. What good does that do?"* (James 2:15-16 NLT) Much like grief in general, we have platitudes to offer that really don't help. Let's be better than that, dear church. It's hard enough to find genuine advice from a Biblical perspective that offers real-world application.

"Okay, I'm supposed to pray that God will lift my depression and focus on scripture and service instead, but I still can't get out of bed in the morning. Do I have unconfessed sin? Am I not praying hard enough? Am I really a Christian?" I've had all of those thoughts. If you're a Christian who has struggled with depression, I bet you have, too.

Maybe you do need to pray harder. Maybe you haven't given yourself enough time to improve. Or maybe you need to act on your behalf physically as well as pray. I have given this example to kids when I teach about prayer: you should pray in faith that God can do anything you ask, but you must still do the things you are responsible for; it's good to pray that God will help you do well on a test, but you have to do your part and study. It's good to pray that God will take away your depression, but you still have to do the work of coping and healing. There is a chicken-and-egg relationship with depression and altered brain chemistry, and sometimes medical intervention to correct the brain chemistry is the best option to begin the healing process. You are not a faith failure for taking an antidepressant if that's what you need to get healthy.

I love that God gave us examples of great people of faith battling depression. He shows us through Biblical examples that we aren't alone or new in this experience. The Psalms are full of songs pouring out depression to God and asking him to fix it. The key we will see in these Psalms, and I believe the key to moving through depression, is to always shift the focus back to higher ground – to God. Even though depression is the opposite of pride, it is equally self-centered and self-destructive. God is the foundation of truth when our emotions lie to us, and we must shift our focus away from the self-centeredness of depression and renew our minds *(Romans 12:2)* to be God-centered. Renewal is hard work, and it requires an active change in your thought patterns.

Let's see how our psalmists expressed and dealt with depression. We'll be reading Psalms 6, 13, 38, 42, 43, 69, 77, 88, 123, 137, 142, and 143. It seems like a lot, but we'll look at several of them together. I also think it's important for us to see that God doesn't hide from depression; he included it in the Bible for us to see. He knows it's part of life and loss, and he gave us examples of real people that he loved living through depression and eventually surviving it. He gave us examples of hope.

Psalm 137

Psalm 137 paints a poignant picture of depression in the first four verses. They sat by the river and wept when they thought about the country they'd lost. They gave up playing music and hung up their harps, refusing to sing in a land that wasn't theirs. The Israelites had been captured and were living in a foreign country; if that isn't the perfect metaphor for grief, I don't know what is. In the face of loss, everything feels different − foreign − as if you're learning how to live again. In this psalm, the Israelites' captors were asking them to sing and play happy songs from their homeland. We may not have physical captors, but we do have demands on our emotions, moments or people that will ask us to sing or act like we did in the time before our grief. For instance, if you have a child, depending on their age, they may not understand why you are sad and need time to be sad. We had a miscarriage about ten months after our daughter was born, and my ten-month-old baby still needed to be fed and cared for and loved. I literally had to sing when all I wanted to do was hang up my harp.

As you think about depression in your life, especially as a reaction to loss, what is the figurative harp that you want to hang up?

What songs are difficult for you to sing – this may not be literal songs, but something that you loved before that's hard to do now without sadness – now that grief has entered the picture?

 Sketch or write about those reflections.

Our psalmist in Psalm 137 vows to never forget Jerusalem, and emphasizes that pledge by cursing themselves if they fail to remember: *"let my right hand forget how to play the harp,"* and *"may my tongue stick to the roof of my mouth." (Psalms 137:5-6 NLT)* It's okay to want to always remember what you lost; in fact, it's a good thing to cherish those memories. It's also completely normal to feel guilty when you begin to sing your songs and play your harp again, whatever that may be in your life. Like this psalmist, we feel as though doing the thing that we vowed not to do in our new landscape of loss betrays the person or thing that we lost. *"How can we sing the songs of the Lord while in a pagan land?" (Psalms 137:4)*

Have you felt like you've betrayed your loss, your sadness, by doing something you used to love?

Did you feel like you might forget if you moved on from depression?

Spend some time looking at what is holding you in this stage. Talk to God about what is keeping you depressed, and ask him to show you ways to still remember while you move forward.

The last few verses of Psalm 137 are a little jarring, and I honestly thought about not addressing them. But I hate it when people try to teach the Bible without addressing the "difficult" parts, so I won't skip over something even if it sounds horrific, like the last verse in particular. I have always loved the Psalms because they are written by "regular" people. Sure, David was a king, but he bares his soul in complete honesty to God. We don't know who wrote all of the psalms, but they weren't all prophets and kings and priests. They were all human, and they were all forthright about their feelings.

This psalmist begged God for vengeance against the Babylonians who destroyed their holy city and took the Israelites captive. Our psalmist was obviously angry, and wished for the most horrible destruction of the Babylonians possible. What the psalmist gets right in these final verses is asking God to remember and avenge the wrong. What he gets wrong, and what we get wrong, is the desire to destroy utterly and avenge ourselves. Destruction of Israel's enemies was always a judgment of God on the enemy country's failure to worship the one true God, and we should always approach such judgment with introspection and solemnity rather than glee at the downfall of our enemy. If your loss came about because of the direct actions of another person, it's tempting to wish for every curse you can call down on them, but pause a moment before you revel in desiring their downfall. Even if you share no blame (the Israelites did own some of the blame for the Babylonian invasion), God calls us to seek justice and to leave the vengeance to him.

Is there some part of your loss you want God to avenge? Ask him here, now to remember how you were wronged and to bring justice if that hasn't happened. Ask him to bring you peace instead of a desire for revenge.

Psalm 38

Psalm 38 was written by David when he was facing grief of his own making. He had sinned and was facing the consequences of that sin. Unlike Psalm 137, in which there is an outside cause of grief, Psalm 38 shows us that we can be grieved over circumstances of our own making. We make a bad decision that alters the course of our lives, and we are left broken and grieving. We don't often find grace or empathy from those around us when we bring about our own depression, but David shows us that we should still face that pain, express it honestly to God, and ask God to forgive us and heal us.

No matter what we have done – don't forget that David committed adultery and murder, and we still consider him to be a beautiful example of faith – Jesus offers us forgiveness and restoration. There will surely be consequences we must face, but we won't face them alone. God will be with us every step of the way.

Have you ever made a mistake that led to loss and grief in your life?

Are you dealing with that now?

Look at your actions honestly, and confess them to Jesus.

Write a prayer asking God to heal you and show you the next steps to take to bring restoration to yourself, to your circumstances, and to the people you may have hurt.

Psalm 88

Psalm 88 is a powerful image of the isolation of depression. Our sadness causes us to withdraw from the people and activities we love; that withdrawal and our depressed mood pushes people away, too, until our withdrawal becomes a vicious cycle of isolation. This psalmist is experiencing acute social isolation, and it is a "trap with no way of escape" if we don't reach out. As an armchair psychologist, I'd venture a guess that this psalmist is experiencing severe, chronic depression. When I was in the midst of chronic depression, I read this psalm and thought, "This is how I feel – God has abandoned me, my family and friends don't really understand what I'm feeling, and darkness is my closest friend. Who would notice if I weren't even here?"

Dear heart, those thoughts are *not* the truth about you or your situation. They are your emotions, and we want to believe our emotions because they are very real and very loud, but emotions are not to be trusted as truth. Emotions are a completely valid reaction, but they are not the truth. You are not your depression, and you can stop the isolation cycle. You have to decide to take some action, though. Depression brain cannot be alleviated without a decision on your part to take some steps to move forward and begin to heal.

Read this psalm again and compare it to your depression. Are you deep in it like our psalmist, or is your depression mild comparatively? Take some time to fully express your emotions – give them words, and let them out.

Once you have written everything out, give yourself permission not to think about it for a day or two. After some time has passed, reread your feelings, and evaluate them by the actual facts of your circumstances. (I don't recommend evaluating right after you've written everything down because that will hurt a bit, and examining emotions is hard work. Allow yourself to rest up and have some space to think other thoughts before you move on to telling truth to your feelings.)

How do your emotions hold up under interrogation?

What steps can you take in light of this revelation to begin healing?

Do you need to reach out to a friend and have a coffee date?

Do you need to exercise regularly?

Do you need to be more consistent in prayer and Bible reading?

Make a plan to put one positive habit into practice every day. Even if it's tempting, don't put too many things on your list at one time so you don't get overwhelmed and fall back into depression brain mode.

Are you still feeling overwhelmed and having trouble telling your feelings the truth?

If you can't see past the emotions at all, and you have been trapped in this stage for more than a few weeks, it's probably time to reach out for help. You are not weak for needing help – at some point, all of us need someone to help carry us through – you are strong for asking for what you need.

Start talking with a friend if you feel uncomfortable talking to a pastor or a therapist. Telling your story out loud to another human will begin to give you some power over it and take some of the sting away with each telling. Just don't stop with talking to a friend if that's not enough to help you see light again. The average friend is not a mental health expert, so there is a limit to how they can help you. If Psalm 88 feels like truth to you even after you've tried to take steps towards healing, please seek professional counseling and talk to your doctor. Sometimes we need extra help to break the depression cycle.

If you're in the deep end of depression, who will you talk to this week to seek help? Pray and ask God to build up your courage to reach out. You can do it. God will be faithful to provide the help that you need, so ask him now.

Psalms 6, 13, 42, 43, 69, and 77

Read Psalms 6, 13, 42, 43, 69, and 77. Compared to the psalms of grief we've read so far, these are a bit different in tone. Where the others have ended still in despair, these psalms transition their focus off the depression and onto God's goodness and faithfulness.

This is the key to being able to speak truth into your circumstances and to shift your mind out of depression brain. I said earlier that depression is very self-centered, and it makes it hard to focus on anything outside our loss and sadness. What these psalmists realized was that they had to purposefully shift their thinking.

Psalm 77 is a great example of how to begin changing the pattern of your thinking. Asaph reminds himself that God is good by recalling and celebrating the things God had done for Israel in the past, from Jacob and Joseph to Moses and Aaron. Even in Asaph's era, this would have been history, but it was a good place to begin expressing gratitude for God's greatness.

In Psalm 69, David ends with thanksgiving and praise for God's historical faithfulness because it means he will redeem his people, including David. Remembering that God is eternally good and faithful will force depression brain to acknowledge that God is unchanging, so God will continue to be good and faithful forever, even to you, even if it doesn't feel like that's what's happening in your life right now.

Gratitude for what God has provided us – despite the loss you are dealing with, you probably have food to eat, a place to live, and at least one friend – is a healthy way to transition out of depression.

Review your life's history. What has God done to take care of you and bring you to this point?

If you are struggling to feel gratitude for anything in your own life, widen your field of view. What in the world around you is there to be thankful for?

Begin wide, and then narrow your thanksgiving to at least one thing specific in your life.

Write a list here of at least five things you are thankful for.

Psalm 143

Read Psalm 143. Read it several more times, and read it aloud. David tells God he is losing all hope, and he will die if God doesn't answer him. Then he asks God to let him hear about his forever love every morning, *"for I am trusting you. Show me where to walk, for I give myself to you." (Psalms 143:8 NLT)*

This is such a healthy model for dealing with depression. David hides none of his feelings from God; in fact, he expresses them all eloquently, but then he also doesn't fail to recognize that God is the source of all goodness and life. He gives himself wholly to God. He trusts God, and he speaks that trust into being.

Read Psalm 143 out loud one more time, and put yourself into it – let it be a prayer from your heart. Spend some time drawing or writing the things God brings to mind as you do this.

Chapter 6 – Acceptance

The last stage in Kubler-Ross's stages of grief is acceptance, which is exactly what it sounds like – a recognition of the facts. Everything to this point has been a struggle, and acceptance is really no less of a fight, despite the word "acceptance." Acceptance is the point when you can mentally and emotionally grasp the reality of your loss; you begin the process of living with it. Having walked intimately with grief for over a decade, I am certain the grief ever goes away. You learn to live with it and to keep moving in your life. The wound becomes less painful, but a scar will always remind you of what you lost – and occasionally, like a broken bone, a good thunderstorm will release a new throb of pain for a while. But you keep moving.

Acknowledging the new reality of your life will enable you to move forward; this will look different in everyone's life. Much as we would like for there to be an exact blueprint to follow, we all have to build where we are with what we have to work with. You will develop a new routine to match the new pattern of your day, and you will find ways to fill the time once consumed by what you are grieving.

I sometimes think of this period in my life as the "Find a Race!" stage because I most often found some sort of endurance race to focus on. After our second miscarriage, I dragged my best friend along on a mission to complete a triathlon; another time I trained for a half marathon. I needed a new goal to focus on so that I could shift my thought patterns from my loss onto something positive I could achieve. I have seen families take on activist roles in combatting the cause of their loved one's death – cancer research, drug abuse rehabilitation, safe driving education – once they accepted the reality of the loss. Their work allowed them to honor the lost loved one and to effect positive change in the lives of other people affected by the same kind of loss. It allowed them to continue to work through their grief in a positive way and acknowledge their "new normal."

A note of advice before you embark on an activist mission closely related to your loss – it's a good idea to wait for an extended period (about a year) before you take on a large role or a counseling role of any kind. You need time and space for your emotional wounds to heal, and putting yourself in a position to reopen them too soon can hinder (or even reverse) your healing process, not to mention the havoc you could wreak on someone else's recovery.

I remember finding a wonderful pregnancy and infant loss support group online that had no Alabama groups available. To start a group, you had to go through their training program, and they very specifically stated that you must not have suffered a pregnancy or infant loss within a year of the training. I was so frustrated that my recurrent miscarriages were preventing me from forming a group that I so desperately needed! After all, I wasn't like everyone else who had suffered through pregnancy loss because I was a "semi-professional" at dealing with it after five or six miscarriages, right? Wrong. I just couldn't see it. I would never have had the emotional stamina to build a support group from the ground up, maintain the leadership stability necessary to keep such a group running, or to cope with the group never coming together if I didn't succeed. I had barely accepted my losses yet, and I wasn't ready for the responsibility of guiding anyone else through grief.

I vividly remember the moment I realized I had truly reached acceptance of our pregnancy losses. Our daughter was three years old, and my husband and I each had our twenty year high school class reunions. On the weekend of my husband's reunion, there was an afternoon picnic at a local park, and everyone was invited to bring their whole family. We fairly constantly fielded the usual questions about children asked at gatherings of old schoolmates: "So is she your only? Do you plan to have more kids?" And the list goes on... I found myself in a conversation with one of my husband's classmates, and I stated very matter-of-factly, "She's our only. We had nine miscarriages before she was born, and one more after she was born, so unless God points us toward adoption, we're done."

There was no bitter inflection, just a statement of facts. The man I was talking to sputtered for a moment and then said, "I'm so sorry. I didn't mean to bring up something so painful." This was the moment I realized my whole perspective had changed. I honestly answered him, "It's not painful to share about now; it's just part of our story." I had been telling our story for some time, but that was the first moment I realized that our story of loss was now just a part of our much bigger story. It finally had perspective and ceased to be the only headline in my life. God had healed my heart enough that I could see his hand guiding me through those long years of loss to a place where I could share our story as an example of God's faithfulness through every trial.

So how do we reach acceptance? We've talked in the previous chapters about dealing with those stages honestly and how to apply healthy and godly coping skills to our emotions. That's most of the hard work that will lead to a statement of facts. At some point in the process of telling truth to your emotions, you'll come to the point where you can bravely and without sharp pain state the facts of your story. You'll acknowledge the pain for what it was, and you'll be able to see what God has done in your life through the healing process.

The ultimate acceptance is being able to look back and see that God not only brought you through your loss, but he also drew you closer to him and taught you to recognize his provision at every point in your journey.

Acceptance may be the last stage in Kubler-Ross's model, but there is nothing final about grief. I find myself slipping back into other stages, especially anger and depression. Reaching a point of acceptance means that I know I won't live in those other stages because I know the truth of my situation and God's hand over it. I know I have at least a few healthy coping mechanisms in my emotional toolbox to work through the mess back to a stable state. Maybe, then, acceptance is like a restore point on a computer – a stable point to return to and to grow from.

Let's read Psalms 30, 65, 90, 103, and 130 to see how the psalmists recorded their moments of acceptance.

Psalm 90

Psalm 90 is a psalm of Moses, and while the end of it tells us Moses hadn't reached the Promised Land with the Israelites yet, the beginning is an excellent statement of facts. You may be reading this and thinking, "This doesn't sound like the uplifting story of acceptance I was expecting." You're right.

Moses was clearly stating mostly negative facts, pointing out that the life of man is full of pain and fleeting. But Moses wasn't hiding from the truth or wallowing in depression: he was expressing the truth of his situation as he realized he would never be entering the land God promised to his people. He was asking for those facts to be a reminder to grow in wisdom and seek forgiveness, which his people were desperately in need of in the years Israel wandered in the desert. To be honest, sometimes our facts suck. Mine do. No one wants to lose ten pregnancies. But I had to be able to state the facts, even (and especially) the ugly ones. Only then could I start to see past them.

What are your facts? Tell your story here in words or pictures.

Psalm 130

Psalm 130 was written for pilgrims traveling to Jerusalem, and it's a lovely continuation of the thought pattern Moses began in Psalm 90. Verse 3 (NLT) says, *"Lord, if you kept a record of our sins, who, O Lord, could survive?"* No matter what the story of our loss is, none of us is perfect, and none of us can stand in God's presence and live because we're not innocent. This psalm points us directly to the character of God's forgiveness as the source of hope and wisdom.

Most of our natural, entirely human, first instincts for coping with our loss are not healthy ones, which means they are sinful. One of my worst habits is to eat to avoid feeling my feelings. The truth of the matter is, what I am doing is a sin because I know better, and I am overeating and not going to God and dealing with hard emotions. Part of acceptance is recognizing the wrong ways we have dealt with our pain for what they are and asking God for forgiveness.

What do you need to face as an unhealthy coping mechanism?

Ask God to use your acknowledgement as a point of acceptance and repentance.

Ask him to use this restore point to teach you deeper wisdom about how to cope with your loss through his grace.

Psalm 30

David shows us a pattern for acceptance in Psalm 30. He begins with his statement of facts in the first three verses, but note that he also acknowledges God's hand in keeping him safe from his enemies and rescuing him from illness and near-death. David recognized that the fact he was still alive meant that God had brought him through those trials and provided for his life. And he called for everyone to join in praising God for turning sadness into joy in verses 4 and 5.

In case we didn't get the point, and because David was a brilliant songwriter, he essentially repeats that same pattern in the last half of the psalm: *"I was broken; I begged you for my life; you delivered me; I will praise you forever."*

You have already stated the facts of your story, so now use David's format to tell your story through the lens of God's mercy. Write a psalm of your own to tell your story as part of God's great story.

Psalm 103

Psalm 103 teaches us that the ultimate acceptance of our loss is to be able to praise God with our whole hearts. I love that David points out that God revealed himself to Moses and then carries Moses's theme of the fleeting life of man to its rightful end. Our lives are short, and our sin is heavy, but God's love is forever and covers our sin with grace.

He ends with a stanza of pure praise. The last line in verse 22 (NLT) tells us everything about acceptance, *"Let all that I am praise the Lord."* All of my healthy, unbroken parts, all of my grief-stricken parts… all of me must praise the Lord.

What does it look like for your whole being to praise God?

Does it even seem possible to praise him with your broken parts?

Play your favorite song of praise to God, and sit, eyes closed, and meditate as you listen or sing along. Bring your attention to every aspect of your life, and intentionally offer it in praise to God as you continue to sing the song. If you feel like your body should be moving, move it as your meditation directs. Feel the Holy Spirit and follow his leading.

Write down or draw your reflections from this meditation so that you can remember what it's like to let all that you are praise the Lord.

Psalm 65

I believe the ultimate acceptance is being able to state the facts of who God is and how he provides for us. No psalm is more direct in that than Psalm 65. Read through this psalm a few times.

 Write a statement of facts about God's character as you have seen him at work in your life.

Chapter 7 – Comfort

Finding comfort at any stage in grief can feel like an impossible feat; I remember praying for God to just give me some instant divine relief, "Just let me feel your arms around me." Sometimes that prayer was answered with a physical hug from someone in my life, but most often God gave me phrases from songs or scripture that soothed my frayed emotions enough to keep moving. It is hard work to accept comfort if you're an independent sort or when you're in the depths of depression, but you need to let in the light of encouragement wherever you can find it. And you must believe the encouraging things people say to you. Depression can whisper – or scream, really – horrible things to you, but that voice isn't the truth. You are a divinely created being worthy of love and respect. You need to hear and accept compliments for what they are – sincere expressions of your value. Don't go it alone. Yes, God is with you, but he created us to share love and community. You need people in your life who will love you and encourage you and share hard truths with you.

One of the things I needed to hear when I questioned God's goodness was that God is God, and I am not. He is in control even when my world is spiraling out of control. Those facts formed a foundation I could build on, and hearing amazing things about God's love added scaffolding around the crumbling bits of my heart. The truth is, whether it feels like it or not, God loves you, and he is for you. He provides for your needs (but not always our wants), and he is present with you even when he feels removed and foreign. He will carry you through this storm and shelter you under his wings like a mother bird; he mourns with you and collects every tear you shed in a bottle; there is no place in creation that God's love cannot reach and pull you out of your pit of despair. You don't have to take my word for it, you can read every one of these promises in the Psalms.

There are no journaling "assignments" in this chapter. There is space after each psalm discussion, so you may write or draw what you discover in these words of comfort, but this section is primarily intended to be encouragement and rest for your soul.

Psalm 20

Psalm 20 is a song of David in the format of a blessing. As you read it, sing this blessing over your life right now, wherever you are on the journey through grief. *"In times of trouble, may the Lord answer your cry. May the name of the God of Jacob keep you safe from all harm. May he send you help from his sanctuary and strengthen you from Jerusalem. May he remember all your gifts and look favorably on your burnt offerings. May he grant your heart's desires and make all your plans succeed. May we shout for joy when we hear of your victory and raise a victory banner in the name of our God. May the Lord answer all of your prayers." (Psalms 20:1-5 NLT)*

God is for you. May your heart remember these blessings pronounced by the "man after God's own heart," by the king anointed and dearly loved by God (as are you, too!). May you never forget that God is for you.

Psalm 23

I think we have all heard Psalm 23 so often that we may take it for granted, but it is certainly worth taking a closer look. Shepherds have the sole responsibility for tending and protecting their flock. I often think of "The Lord is my shepherd," as, "The Lord is my guide." I don't know why my brain has limited the role of shepherd to merely leading the flock from one place to another, when in reality, they watch over the sheep to protect them and ensure that they have good pasture and plentiful fresh water as well as keep them together on the path in transit.

What better protector and provider could there be for a sheep than the all-knowing, all-powerful, all-present God? It's no coincidence that the first things mentioned that the shepherd provides are rest and peace. If God is for you – and he is – then you can let him take over guard duty for your life and rest in his strength. A sheep under the protection of the One True God can be assured that there is nowhere too dark for Jesus to cast his light, nothing too scary for his power to vanquish.

Something else I often overlook in this beautiful picture of how God cares for his people is found in verse 6: *"Surely your goodness and unfailing love will pursue me all the days of my life..." (NLT)* Not just, "You'll love me forever," but "You will pursue me forever." You are so greatly loved that God will not only never stop loving you, but he will also never stop pursuing you. Some other words for "pursue" are "woo," "encourage," "chase," "entice." You don't encourage or woo or entice something of no value; you only chase after something worthy and immensely valuable. You, dear friend, are worthy of pursuit by the Creator of the world.

Psalm 33

Psalm 33 is a beautiful declaration of who God is and how wonderfully he knows us. If you are struggling like I did to hold on to faith – to decide if your faith is based on anything true when it feels like your world is unraveling at light speed – then hold on to this psalm. *"For the word of the Lord holds true, and we can trust everything he does."* *(Psalms 33:4 NLT)*

This song reminds us that God only had to speak to create the world and that his plans can never be shaken. I think what I love most about this psalm is the reminder that God understands my heart intimately because he made it. Grief can be isolating because we struggle to make our hearts known to those around us, and we feel misunderstood, invisible, and unheard. I promise you that God sees you. He knows your heart. He understands you, and he will surround your heart with his great love.

Psalm 46

As we look at Psalm 46, I have to tell you that sometimes I see something absurd that no one else does until you point it out. In this case, after you have read Psalm 46, go back and look closely at the directions given to the choir director. This psalm talks about a lot of destruction and feels a little warrior-like to me, and the choir director is instructed that it is to be sung by soprano voices. I really feel like there should be some baritone involved if mountains are falling into the sea, but maybe that's just me. Now that you have silly musical instructions in your head (See, Bible study is fun!), listen to what the words are singing to you (in whatever range is pleasing to your ear, though soprano is obviously recommended).

Here is what stands out to me: "God is our refuge," "God dwells in that city; it cannot be destroyed," "The Lord of Heaven's Armies is here among us." These are all military defense terms describing God as a fortress, a safe place, a stronghold amid the chaos. If everything around you is war and chaos, run to the fortress and find peace from the mess outside. Rest in the knowledge that if God dwells in you, you cannot be destroyed. Once you hide your heart and soul in the refuge of the Lord, you can breathe and be still. *"Be still, and know that I am God!" (Psalms 46:10a NLT)* I love that we must be still and know. We don't get to keep running and worrying and battling and know; we must be still and rest to know that God is God.

Psalm 50

In Psalm 50, we have an image of God calling all of the people on earth together for a time of judgement. He tells the faithful that he is their God and that he has no complaint about their sacrifices. Then he tells them that he has no need for the physical things his people offer as sacrifices; thankfulness is the sacrifice he desires from us. I don't know about you, but I am a try-harder, make-a-to-do-list-to-make-it-happen kind of person. Everything about what God says he wants here feels like it's just too easy. What do you mean all you want is thankfulness? I am tithing and volunteering, and serving, and... None of that is necessary to be loved and accepted by God.

All we have to do to be rescued by God is to trust him and to thank him for his grace. In this time of judgement, God asks the wicked why they even try to act religious when they ignore his words and treat other people badly. But their story doesn't have to end there – God offers them relief from judgement if they repent, promising again that thankfulness is the best sacrifice we can offer. God doesn't need us to do incredible feats of strength or to uphold strict religious standards to please him. He only wants us to be grateful for what he's done for us. It may be simple work, but living a life of gratitude is radically different from the standards the world wants to impose on us. The best part of making thanksgiving your work is that by following the standards God set forth, he will reveal salvation to us.

Psalm 56

Psalms 56:8 was probably the single most comforting verse in the Bible to me when I couldn't stop crying. The New Living Translation reads this way: *"You keep track of all my sorrows. You have collected all my tears in your bottle. You have recorded each one in your book."*

There are a lot of other truths about God being on our side in Psalm 56, but this verse was a lifeline for me. I felt alone and insignificant and worn out from crying, and I was sure no one else could know exactly how much my heart ached. I felt like God had abandoned me or maybe had even cursed me to a life of unending grief. And then I read this promise. God has a record of every sorrow that has wounded my heart. He has a bottle with every tear I have shed in it. He never forgot about me, even when he felt a million miles away.

God's desire is never for us to suffer, but horrible things will happen on this earth that is broken by sin. Our suffering is never ignored or wasted. Sometimes we will get to see God use it here on earth – my suffering was transformed into writing as a way to share hope with others – but we can be sure that even if we can't see God use our suffering for good here on earth, he has a record of it and it will be redeemed in heaven. You'll see the full glory of God and the whole reach of your story in the kingdom of heaven. I promise you that what we know about here on earth is only a fraction of God's story. If you are faithful to let him use your suffering to draw you close to him, he will be faithful to transform it into his brilliant glory. If Jesus turned plain old water into wine, imagine what God will do with your tears.

Psalm 62

Psalm 62 is a song of David declaring that God is his fortress and his rock. David says several times in this psalm that he will wait quietly in the presence of God. We saw in Psalm 46 that quiet means we must rest from struggling and be still. What I also see in David's confidence that he can wait quietly is that God already knows about the storms surrounding us, so there's no need to frantically try to get God's attention. We are already safe and unshakeable if we have made God our fortress and source of salvation.

David felt so confident and secure that he was on solid ground and protected that he tells everyone, *"O my people, trust in him at all times. Pour out your heart to him, for God is our refuge." (Psalms 62:8 NLT)* Pour out your heart to God and know that he will guard it. There is no need for you to build your own fortress walls around your heart because it is already surrounded by the solid rock of Jesus, through whom we have salvation and eternal victory.

Psalm 68

Psalm 68 is a song of praise for what God has done for Israel by saving them from slavery in Egypt and establishing them safely as a nation with a permanent temple for God in Jerusalem. Simply praising God and thanking him for what he's done in the past can be comforting when we can't see good in our current circumstances of grief. Read verses 5 and 6 again. "Father to the fatherless, defender of widows — this is God." Your grief may be an emotional prison, but the God who takes care of the fatherless and widowed will also set you free and fill you with joy. It's in his character; he just can't help it. His desire is for us to be perfect, which means whole and complete, lacking nothing, just as God is perfect.

Now read verse 19 again. Our savior God carries us in his arms every day. Not just in hard times. Every. Day. God doesn't expect us to be strong on our own on an easy day, so he surely isn't expecting us to be strong by ourselves when we're coping with loss. Not only does God carry us through it in his strength, he will place us in his family so that there will be people to journey with. We aren't meant to be alone or socially isolated. The family of God is intended to be support here on earth and not just in heaven. This is the power of the church when we act like the Body of Christ.

Psalm 91

If you are feeling attacked on every side, stop and read Psalm 91 out loud. It may feel silly, but there is something powerful about saying words aloud and hearing them spoken, even if you are both the reader and the audience. Listen to God's promise to you that he is your shelter, your rest, your strong fortress, your safety, your armor, your rescue.

It may feel like evil is overtaking you, but if you make God your refuge, nothing can touch your salvation. Your eternity is secure in Christ, and the evils that befall you on earth will be avenged by God himself. Look closely at the imagery in verse 4: *"He will cover you with his feathers. He will shelter you with his wings. His faithful promises are your armor and protection." (NLT)* This isn't the only place in the Bible that describes God gathering his people under his wings to cover and protect them. It calls to mind a mother bird gathering her chicks under her wing to protect them from the elements and from animals of prey. The act is tender and life sustaining. This is our God, waiting to scoop you up and pull you in close.

Psalm 93

Psalm 93 has always danced into song in my heart when I read it, it's so majestic and certain. It's also short and straight to the point: God is the king over all creation, and he cannot be overthrown by any circumstance. In the midst of loss, it feels like our world is shattered and nothing is sure. *"The world stands firm and cannot be shaken,"* *(Psalms 93:1b NLT)* because God is, as he has always been and always will be, firmly on his throne. He will never change, and he is holy forever. No matter what is happening around us – no matter how high the flood waters rise or how loudly the seas roar – God is in control.

Psalm 104

Psalm 104 creates so many beautiful images that are worth savoring and spending time just praising God for his faithfulness and his provision along with the psalmist. I love the picture of God wearing a robe of light and stretching out a curtain of stars! The way this psalmist tells the story of creation is so rich and vivid in every detail, and each line serves to point out how God provides for everything he creates. God loves to create and breathe life, and you are no exception. He takes pleasure in giving you life and purpose, and he will provide for your needs. Even in our pain, this is true, and we can rejoice. You are created by God; he will care for you forever.

Psalm 112

It can be hard to believe that Psalm 112 is true when your world is upside down, especially if we interpret this psalm as a promise of monetary wealth and worldly success. We are promised the wealth of God if we follow him and live with open hands. Our natural instinct when we face loss it to hold on tightly to the things we think we own or control; we think we can protect those things from being taken from us if we hold on tightly enough. God reminds us in this psalm that he is the source of our wealth and our success, and he calls us to share freely. Especially when we feel out of control, we need to open our hands to let go of our claim on earthly things so that we can claim God's promise of eternal things that can never be taken away from us.

Psalm 116

Psalm 116 is full of encouragement from a psalmist who has lived through "trouble and sorrow." There are two places I want to draw your attention. First, look at the first two verses. God hears your voice, and he *bends down* to listen: he makes an effort to listen to you. Our psalmist responded to that knowledge with a declaration to pray as long as he had breath. That seems like a completely reasonable reaction. The maker of the world wants to hear from you, and he will come down to you so he can listen closely to your heart. It reminds me of a parent leaning in to listen to a child's small voice so they can be sure to catch every word.

I also want to be sure that you look again at verse 15: *"The Lord cares deeply when his loved ones die." (NLT)* It's hard to imagine that God would care much when his people die on earth since we know we will live for eternity in his presence in heaven. But we get the idea from this verse that he is saddened by the earthly loss in spite of the eternal quality of our souls. God isn't absent in our mourning – he cares very much about our loss. I can't express how it lifted my heart to know that God cared deeply about each baby we lost. I don't know what it looks like in heaven, but we can be sure God mourns with us.

Psalm 121

I have sung the words in Psalm 121 in some form in every single choir I have been a part of since elementary school. "Slumbers not nor sleeps" can be a tongue twister, and it always felt like a silly redundancy. However, the repetition works as a literary device to emphasize the fact that God is never asleep at the wheel. He is always watching over you and protecting you, day and night, *"as you come and go, both now and forever."* *(Psalms 121:8 NLT)* Psalm 23 establishes God as our shepherd whose job it is to protect us. This psalm tells us that his protection detail never ends, and he never loses sight of us. As humans we can't imagine never sleeping on a watch post – that's why we set several guard shifts overnight. God doesn't have a second watch or third watch because he never slumbers at his post.

Psalm 139

Psalm 139 was a bit like a mantra for me after each miscarriage. In the first stanza, David praises God for his intimate knowledge of us. He knows our heart inside and out; he knows our every action and word before we even form the idea in our brains. Then David goes on to proclaim that there is nowhere on earth, above it in the heavens, or below it in the grave where we can hide from God's presence. And nothing can hide us from him.

There is no darkness that God can't see through and light up – not even the darkness of death or depression. You are always firmly in God's hands, and his lovingkindness is always with you.

Verses 13 through 16 are what kept me glued together when my soul felt fractured and lost in grief. God made each and every one of us, and he knew us before we were even conceived. He has numbered our days, and every moment is recorded in God's book. My babies, no matter how brief their lives were in my womb, are no exception to this. God's workmanship is unrivaled, and we are each a beloved work of art created by the master craftsman. And we can be sure that not one of us will leave this life before God's story for us is finished.

Psalm 147

Psalm 147 praises God for protecting his people and providing for them. The main reason I chose this psalm to share with you for comfort is found in verses 2 through 4. This psalm of praise was written after Jerusalem had been captured and destroyed, and the people of Israel were led away in captivity. From an earthly perspective, all was lost. They had no homeland, no temple in which to worship and sacrifice, no hope of returning to the life they knew before in their promised land. They were deep in loss. Eventually, circumstances changed, and the Israelites were allowed to return to Jerusalem and rebuild the city – first the city walls, then homes, and then the temple.

God restored them after their loss. It didn't wipe out their grief; the past was still the past, and the exile would remain part of their history. But God brought them back and gave them new dreams to replace the lost promise.

"He heals the brokenhearted and bandages their wounds." (Psalms 147:3 NLT) Have you ever imagined God as a triage nurse? Yet here he is described as exactly that, binding our wounds and helping us to heal, easing the pain little by little, protecting our wounds until they are less tender and able to be exposed to the environment. You will heal in time, and God is working to wrap your wounds in his love while you work through the healing process. The God who created all the stars, put them into their places, and knows all their names – that's the God who is also putting bandages on the broken places of your heart. If creating and naming every star wasn't too big a task, he is surely able to bring peace and healing to your pain.

Chapter 8 – Forgive

An aspect of depression and grief that we may tend to overlook or gloss over is forgiveness. There can be a lot of guilt in loss – you blame yourself, you blame someone else for causing your loss, you blame God for allowing the loss to happen, and then you feel guilty for all the finger pointing you're doing or the anger you're feeling. We say silly things like, "You have to forgive yourself," but how do you really do that? What if you really have done horrible things because you were acting on your emotions? What if you really have damaged other people or relationships because of your words or actions (or lack thereof) when you were depressed? See? Lots of guilt. Not lots of grace.

All the things we do that are less than perfect are sin. Sin is anything – behavior or attitude or belief – that is unequal to God's standard, which is perfection. The only human who has ever lived without sin is Jesus. You are not Jesus. I am not Jesus. We have all sinned. That's the bad news; the good news is that God is always faithful to forgive us when we ask. And when we ask for his forgiveness, he wipes our slate clean – that sin is gone forever, removed from us as far as the east is from the west (Psalms 103:12). You may feel like the idea of forgiving yourself is completely unlike the forgiveness of sins, but I think we need to see it in the same light. We'll dive into that more deeply when we look at Psalm 32.

Forgiving yourself is hard work, and we need to begin with forgiving other people if we're going to succeed at giving ourselves the same grace. Grief, loss, and depression feel largely self-centered once you finally begin to gain perspective and see past the fog of those emotions, but our experience of the pain of loss can also focus heavily on what others say and do to us.

Very often, we feel that people say things intentionally to hurt us, or we perceive their actions (or inactions) to be a direct threat or insult. When I am hurting, I see everything that happens to me as piling on – my husband didn't like what I cooked for dinner, so I must be a horrible cook and a terrible person (even though he just doesn't like turkey meatballs…); no one asked for my input about a project at work, so they must think I inept or too far behind to be of any help (even though I really needed the space to catch up and didn't really need to be part of the discussion…); some idiot at the grocery store asked me when we're going to have another baby (even though I don't know this person, so their opinion is completely irrelevant to my life…). Most of the time, my grievances have nothing to do with the person who "wronged" me and everything to do with my emotional state. Occasionally, I have reason to take offense, but then I must follow up on that in a way that honors Christ.

In the instances when I am offended, but there is no reason for the other person to apologize (who can blame my husband for disliking turkey meatballs??), I still have to forgive them in order to let go of the anger their "offense" caused in my heart. I must let go of that so that I can let go of any grudge I am tempted to hold onto and nurse because it makes me feel better to be righteously indignant. When every perceived slight you experience causes you deep emotional pain, you need to evaluate what the source of that pain really is and let go of the hurt and anger you're feeling that is misdirected. You can walk around being offended by everyone and everything, but you'll be an angry, bitter person who begins to alienate people when what you need most is to be comforted by people.

Start with the small things and make a habit of mentally forgiving the offense and immediately dropping it. This takes practice because, if you're anything like me, the offensive thing will keep popping into your head. Each time, I have to remind myself that it is forgiven, and I have to let it go.

I have a few rules that I apply to whether I address a grievance or not. The first rule is whether the person who aggrieved me matters to me. Rude cashier who can't help but comment on every single purchase I make? Doesn't matter. Forgive and don't waste breath trying to explain how she offended me. A friend or family member I have a real relationship with and would like to have a deeper relationship with? They are worth the conversation every time, but I must approach the topic when I am no longer angry and can explain why I was hurt. Most of the time, that person didn't even realize that what they said or did was offensive to me. Most of the time a good conversation without anger leads to a healed relationship and a deeper bond of trust. And then you should forgive and move on.

The second rule is one I learned in puppy training school: addressing a problem too long after the fact doesn't do any good. This one is twofold for me; if after some time has passed, I'm not still angry, then I never address it and just let it go; if I waited for a long time after an offense and never addressed it, then I have lost the right to bring it up again – so let it go. I am awful at this rule when it comes to arguing or being angry at someone I have a long history with, but I did at least learn in marriage counseling that this is a terribly unfair way to fight and is toxic for everyone involved. I practice hard at letting go of things and only addressing the issue at hand.

Honestly, I now find fewer things that I have the energy or desire to pursue later. Almost every time I find myself offended, a little bit of time and space lets me see that I was really worked up over nothing. That hasn't always been the case, and I carried a lot of anger directed at everyone for a long time. I was angry at my doctors for not finding a problem or not testing for enough things. I was angry at anyone who said something stupid in an effort to be comforting. I was angry at anyone who called me on mistakes and turned it into an issue about them and not me. I was angry at women who were walking through the grocery store for being pregnant or for being in my line of sight with their babies. I wanted someone to blame for my misery, so I blamed everyone.

The reality is, God never promised any of us an easy time on earth, and some of you have experienced more pain and more junk than I can even begin to comprehend. I don't know why. It is horrible, and I hate that you have experienced such pain. I do know that God is still bigger than all our messes and all of our circumstances, and he forgives us. And he calls us to forgive others whether they ask for our forgiveness or not. He's pretty persistent about this point. Here are just a few things Jesus said about forgiving others, one while he was dying on a cross:

"If you forgive those who sin against you, your heavenly Father will forgive you. But if you refuse to forgive others, your Father will not forgive your sins." Matthew 6:14-15 NLT

"Then Peter came to him and asked, 'Lord, how often should I forgive someone who sins against me? Seven times?' 'No, not seven times,' Jesus replied, 'but seventy times seven!'" Matthew 18:21-22 NLT

"Jesus said, 'Father, forgive them, for they don't know what they are doing.'" Luke 23:34a NLT

Still not convinced? Here is advice Paul gave to the early church about how to treat each other:

"Get rid of all bitterness, rage, anger, harsh words, and slander, as well as all types of evil behavior. Instead be kind to each other, tenderhearted, forgiving one another, just as

God through Christ has forgiven you." Ephesians 4:31-32 NLT

"Make allowance for each other's faults, and forgive anyone who offends you. Remember, the Lord forgave you, so you must forgive others." Colossians 3:13 NLT

I love this last verse because it reminds me that forgiveness isn't about the person who offended you; it's about your relationship with God. Jesus forgave me, so I must forgive. I wish I had an easy way to forgive and forget, but alas I am human. My best advice is to redirect your thought process when you remember an offense or are tempted to hold a grudge. If you have forgiven the person, change the conversation in your head about that person or event: "It's forgiven, so I choose to think about her smile instead." Eventually the thing will pop into your mind less frequently, and you will be able to think of something positive instead of how you were hurt. For the record, this takes great effort, and I still often stink at this, but every time I put my grievances into the perspective of God's forgiveness, I realize I am wrong to carry around such hurt and anger. Also for the record, I have some beautiful friendships that would not exist if I had walked away just because I got my feelings hurt. I'm so grateful that my family and friends choose to forgive me, too. Relationships are worth the effort, and a relationship with Christ is worth the act of forgiving others.

While we're forgiving others, (I know this will sound sacrilegious to some, but I will venture ahead anyway...): we must forgive God.

I experienced loss for which no one was to blame. I had ten miscarriages, and no cause was discovered for most of them – no disease, no external cause – nothing. I had no place to direct blame; there was no discernable cause for my loss – not cancer, not addiction, not car wrecks, not old age... Only God – who could have stopped it, who could have stopped every single miscarriage from happening. I watched other women experience scares in their pregnancies, but each one of them ended in a miraculous save by God. Where was my miracle? Why wasn't I loved enough by God for him to at least answer my prayer to leave me barren if I was destined to lose every baby that attached itself to my uterus? How could a God who let me lose ten babies be good and loving? He was anything but kind to me. Maybe he didn't directly cause my miscarriages, but he could have stopped them, and that's almost the same thing as causing them if God is omnipotent, right?

I thought all of those things. I thought my faith must not be strong enough because my prayers were going unanswered while I saw miracles happen around me. I hated God. I was so angry I couldn't talk to him, I couldn't read the Bible, and I couldn't sing in church if I even went at all. We church people say a lot of stupid things when we try to comfort people who have suffered traumatic loss: "It's all part of God's plan," "It was just God's timing," and my favorite, "It will all work out when he wants it to." So, he didn't want ten of my pregnancies to work out?!? God *PLANNED* for me to suffer like this?!? No, thanks. I'm going to rethink everything I know about God while you spout churchy words at me because that does *NOT* sound like a merciful God to me.

I had no idea what to do with the anger I felt toward God, so I turned to a Bible study book about dealing with pregnancy and infant loss. I only got more frustrated when the author said in one chapter that it's okay to be mad at God and then said that being angry at God is a sin in the next chapter. I may have burned that book... The thing is, the author wasn't all wrong.

Being angry at God isn't a sin, but what you do with that anger might be. I love reading the Psalms because they are written by people who poured out their whole hearts to God. There's plenty of anger and plenty of blaming God, but there's also the realization that God is unshakeable, unchanging, and undeniable. It is okay to be angry at God and to tell him you are angry; it is not okay to live in that anger and let it dictate your actions. Only your faith should do that.

The Bible has pretty simple guidelines for anger: *"And 'don't sin by letting anger control you.' Don't let the sun go down while you are still angry, for anger gives a foothold to the devil." (Ephesians 4:26-27 NLT)*

We do stupid stuff when we're angry – well, I do; you are probably more mature than I am and can hold your temper. When anger controls you, you will act more rashly and more harshly than you should, and you will do something you'll regret once you calm down. Those angry actions and words are what's sinful – not the anger itself. So be angry at God if you need to, but then you should dump it all out and tell him everything and forgive him – let it go.

The hard truth is we do not deserve anything but judgment from God's hand. I am a sinner (I am not perfect like God is perfect), and the consequence of my sin is God's judgment and my death. We live in a world full of sin where horrible things happen because of our sin, and while God intervenes sometimes, we are not owed any miracles. While we live on this earth, we will suffer because the world is broken and in desperate need of a savior to make it whole and perfect again. But God is still God; he is always good and just and merciful. He is still in control, and he still loves you, no matter what your circumstances seem to tell you. And he loves you no matter how you have sinned.

Living in anger "gives a foothold to the devil" by allowing you to think that God owes you something or that your suffering has earned you the right to demand things from God. Don't let anger narrow your focus to the one thing you didn't get from God. Look around you at what he has provided, and be grateful you haven't gotten the punishment you truly deserve.

Once I stopped being angry and forgave God, I regained the relationship with him I'd been missing. I realized that I didn't have the babies I so desperately wanted, but he had provided for all of my physical needs; he gave me a kind and wonderful husband; he gave me nurturing family and friends; and he gave me purpose. Forgiving God wasn't about God at all, but it was entirely about my relationship with him and how I viewed myself in light of his forgiveness of my sins.

If you're feeling angry at God, you're not going to hell for feeling angry. You're actually in good company since David, who wrote a lot of the Psalms and expressed anger at God, was called a man after God's own heart. But stay in that company and follow David's example: lay it all out before God, and then realize that he is God, and he's got this. He's got you. Don't miss out on a relationship with your creator because you're mad.

This chapter on forgiveness would be incomplete without this final part – be forgiven. Forgiveness in our lives is all modeled on the forgiveness of Jesus in the form of his death as a sacrifice for all of our sins (our less-than-perfect moments). Even in the Torah and books of the prophets in what Christians call the Old Testament, a blood sacrifice was required to cover sins and make people righteous in God's eyes. The very first sin of Adam and Eve required a blood sacrifice that God himself prepared for them by killing animals and using their skins to cover Adam and Eve's nakedness when they left the Garden of Eden. Other religions view less-than-perfection differently, and many see good and evil like a balance scale where enough good to outweigh the bad makes things right.

This is a noble way to see good and evil, but it leaves a lot of gaps for me intellectually and spiritually. How much good is enough to make up for the bad in my life? Is there a ratio of good to bad that will ensure that I will be a good enough person to go to heaven? Is 2:1 enough, or should it be more like 10:1? What is the standard for my good acts – are small acts of kindness like compliments enough to make up for losing my temper? What if I do something worse, like kill someone – what can possibly make up for that on the scale? If enough people put good mojo out into the world, will it ever be enough good to keep horrible things from happening? If everyone on the planet could pay it forward for a day or a week, could we keep earthquakes at bay or stop mass shootings? How much good karma would it take to prevent bad karma from happening at all? If I can repeat my life through multiple reincarnations, could I ever be good enough to make it heaven, or will I be stuck in an endless loop of repeating my less-than-perfection?

The problem with all of these beliefs for me is that the focus is always on self – what can *you* do to earn a place in heaven? Any system based solely on your actions is a meritocracy, and you must work your way into heaven. The worst part of this for me is that there are no clear guidelines for just how good you must be, and there are no real explanations for why evil exists or why bad things happen to good people. As badly as Christians often explain it, God does provide a foundation for these questions I have about a meritocratic heaven.

Heaven isn't a meritocracy; there's nothing you can do to earn it because grace is a gift of God given with no strings attached except to follow Jesus. There is a clear standard for perfection and sin, and there is a clear consequence for sin. Sin is anything less than perfection in our thoughts and actions, and the consequence of sin is death (separation from God forever). The only way to regain our connection to the Creator of our souls is to accept the sacrifice of Jesus and allow him to lead us through life on earth. In exchange, our relationship with God is restored, and we will live forever with our Creator in heaven when our bodies pass away. No earning our way to perfection; no earning a place in heaven, because it is a gift of God. Our good works are the result of following Jesus.

Because sin entered our world, our world is broken as well; things will never be perfect here like they were in the Garden of Eden until God makes the whole world new. Until that happens, bad things will happen no matter how good we are or how well we imitate Jesus. Evil is loose in our world, and we can't do enough good deeds to wipe it out. Only Jesus can eradicate evil. God's grace saves us from condemnation, but it doesn't exempt us from experiencing evil here on earth.

Here are some passages of the Bible that I think tie up the old system of animal sacrifice for sin with the new promise made through Jesus's sacrifice of his life for ours.

"In fact, according to the law of Moses, nearly everything was purified with blood. For without the shedding of blood, there is no forgiveness. That is why the Tabernacle and everything in it, which were copies of things in heaven, had to be purified by the blood of animals. But the real things in heaven had to be purified with far better sacrifices than the blood of animals. For Christ did not enter into a holy place made with human hands, which was only a copy of the true one in heaven. He entered into heaven itself to appear now before God on our behalf. And he did not enter heaven to offer himself again, like the high priest here on earth who enters the Most Holy Place year after year with the blood of an animal. If that had been necessary, Christ would have had to die again and again, ever since the world began. But now, once for all time, he has appeared at the end of the age to remove sin by his own death as a sacrifice." Hebrews 9:22-26 NLT

"When Adam sinned, sin entered the world. Adam's sin brought death, so death spread to everyone, for everyone sinned. Yes, people sinned even before the law was given. But it was not counted as sin because there was not yet any law to break. Still, everyone died – from the time of Adam to the time of Moses – even those who did not disobey an explicit commandment of God, as Adam did. Now Adam is a symbol, a representation of Christ, who was yet to come. But there is a great difference between Adam's sin and God's gracious gift. For the sin of this one man, Adam, brought death to many. But even greater is God's wonderful grace and his gift of forgiveness to many through this other man, Jesus Christ. And the result of God's gracious gift is very different from the result of that one man's sin. For Adam's sin led to condemnation, but God's

119

free gift leads to our being made right with God, even though we are guilty of many sins." Romans 5:12-16

This sounds like a lot of religious mumbo-jumbo, and I guess maybe it is. The bottom line for me is that I don't want to be my own standard bearer; if I am a standard for goodness, I am a miserable example, and there is no hope for humanity. I have looked long and hard into my own soul, and I know what darkness lives there. I think I'm a pretty good person, so if I can see such darkness in me, I have no hope of doing enough good deeds to earn a place in heaven.

Jesus for me means freedom from myself and my darkness. He told us, *"Come to me, all of you who are weary and carry heavy burdens, and I will give you rest. Take my yolk upon you. Let me teach you, because I am humble and gentle at heart, and you will find rest for your souls. For my yoke is easy to bear, and the burden I give you is light." (Matthew 11:28-30 NLT)* Jesus offers release from the relentless burden of myself and my less-than-perfections. He offers me rest for my soul, and I desperately want and need that respite.

We'll be looking at Psalms 32, 51, 80, and 126 to begin working through forgiveness.

Psalm 32

Read Psalm 32. The first five verses in the NLT are: *"Oh, what joy for those whose disobedience is forgiven, whose sin is put out of sight! Yes, what joy for those whose record the Lord has cleared of guilt, whose lives are lived in complete honesty! When I refused to confess my sin, my body wasted away, and I groaned all day long. Day and night your hand of discipline was heavy on me. My strength evaporated like water in the summer heat. Finally, I confessed all my sins to you and stopped trying to hide my guilt. I said to myself, 'I will confess my rebellion to the Lord.' And you forgave me! All my guilt is gone."*

I love reading this psalm because of the physical imagery of a body wasting away and groaning all day long. The image is visceral and heavy and painful to imagine, and I have felt that way over unconfessed sin. I have felt that way in depression over every single mistake I made in a given day; I wouldn't be able to go to sleep because I replayed every word, every step, and judged whether I should have said or done something differently. Whether or not God's hand of discipline was heavy, mine certainly was. All the time. I've described a little bit of my inner voice and how horrible it could be. I judged pretty much everything I said or did to be the wrong thing, and I hated pretty much everything about me all the time — too fat, too out of shape, too angry, too lazy, too loud, too short, too inefficient, too busy, too far behind to ever catch up, bad at mothering, horrible at wifing, ridiculously awful at housekeeping... I couldn't forgive myself for anything because everything was all my fault.

Now I can see how self-centered that is and how unrealistically hard I was on myself. It only got better with forgiveness and medication. The medicine knocked the edge off the irritability enough to allow me to view my circumstances with less anger and bigger perspective. I could see past myself enough to see God and others more clearly. So I confessed my sins to God, and he forgave me. Then I admitted all of my real shortcomings (I say real to emphasize that some of the things I felt guilty about in depressive episodes were imagined flaws.) to myself, and I decided that if God can clear my record of guilt I must clear myself of guilt. After all, I am not Jesus, and if Jesus decides to forgive me, do I really think I know better than him? Not forgiving myself was an act of rebellion because it was a way of putting myself before God.

It's not always that simple in practice, but my inner critic is much quieter these days. I try to be nicer to myself and realize that I will never be perfect on earth, but I can always count on God to forgive me. I try not to be so hard on myself and to focus more on what I got right each day than what I got wrong. I don't let myself off the hook without some examination because I do need to find the roots of my sin and work to bring them in line with the perfection of Christ, but I do admit now that I am human. When I find my self-talk shifting back into guilt mode, I make an effort to stop that train of thought and say something nice to myself instead. And do you know what? I am strong, I am smart, I am kind, I am beautiful, and (most importantly) I am a loved child of God. I feel a hundred pounds lighter knowing that I am forgiven, not because I earned it, but only because God loves me. *"Shout for joy, all you whose hearts are pure!" (Psalms 32:11 NLT)*

How about you? What do you need to talk to God about and then let go of to forgive yourself?

What guilt do you dwell on?

What does your inner critic sound like?

Aren't you ready to shout for joy?

Psalm 51

Let's look at Psalm 51. David wrote this psalm of confession and repentance after a prophet named Nathan came and confronted David about his affair with Bathsheba. David hadn't been able to admit his sin and deal with it until he was confronted with it. God used Nathan to tell David that his adultery hadn't gone unnoticed and that avoiding it and pretending that everything was just fine was not fine with God. Sin was keeping David from fulfilling God's purposes in his life. Most importantly, it was an unavoidable wedge in his relationship with God.

Our job on earth is always to love God and to make him known; we can't do that if something is getting in the way of our communication with God. Psalm 51 is a wonderful template for confessing our sins and restoring our relationship.

David went straight to the heart of repentance in the opening lines of the psalm: *"Have mercy on me, O God, because of your unfailing love." (Psalms 51:1 NLT)* David recognizes the proper order of the relationship God has established for us by asking God to step back into the primary position. David was a king, so he had the power to show mercy to his subjects if they asked for forgiveness. Begging for God to show mercy acknowledges that God is David's king. When we refuse to acknowledge God's proper place as the king of our hearts, we are usurping his authority; we're basically doing the same thing Lucifer did to be thrown out of heaven, the same thing that got Adam and Eve kicked out of Eden, the same thing that got David in this particular mess... You see the pattern here, right?

Do you struggle to let God have authority over your whole life?

Why do you think it's so hard?

Spend some time now asking God to help you submit to his authority and confessing the sin that results when you don't. Write out or draw what your life looks like with you in charge, and then sketch out what it looks like under God's authority.

David goes on to ask God to purify him from his sins and clean him "whiter than snow." Once we confess our sins, God is faithful to wash them away from our souls, never to be seen again. One of my favorite pastimes is soaking in a hot bath. The feeling when I get out is luxuriously squeaky clean. That's the promise of repentance: God will take away every spot of darkness from our souls, clean our hearts, and give us back our pure joy in him.

 Imagine soaking in a tub of God's grace. Write or draw what comes to mind.

Over and over in the psalms and through his prophets, God tells his people that what he really desires as sacrifices from his people aren't animals but thankfulness, humbled hearts, and love for one another. We see that theme here again at the end of Psalm 51. *"The sacrifice you desire is a broken spirit. You will not reject a broken and repentant heart, O God." (Psalms 51:17 NLT)*

God wants our recognition that he alone is good and worthy of our praise. He wants our broken hearts so that he can bind them up and make them whole and good like him. He will never reject our brokenness and our confessions. He will never belittle us or punish us for coming to him humble and imperfect. God will accept your sacrifice as pure and holy and sacred if you bring him a heart waiting for him. We so often think of sacrifices as something of great value, like the animals prescribed in the Old Testament for sin offerings and tithes, or even as great epic tasks around Lent.

Does this idea of sacrifice line up with what God consistently tells us he wants?

Are you willing to change your idea of sacrifice to match his?

What does it look like in your life to offer God a sacrifice?

Psalm 80

Read Psalm 80. Over and over Asaph repeats, *"Turn us again to yourself, O God. Make your face shine down upon us. Only then will we be saved." (Psalms 80:3 and 7 and 19 NLT)* Coverage is a central theme throughout the Bible: Adam and Eve had to be covered physically with clothing after they sinned; their sin had to be covered with a blood sacrifice; the procedure established for atoning for sins was blood sacrifice that covered the altar in the temple; God's physical presence in the mercy seat inside the holy of holies in the temple had to be covered; God covered the eyes of Moses when he appeared to him in person; Jesus covered our sins with his sacrifice to end the necessity for animal sacrifice.

The thing about sin is it covers us up. It hides us from the presence of God and separates us from him. God's face can no longer shine down upon us when we have sin lying down on top of us. It feels desperate, like Asaph does in this psalm, because we can't uncover ourselves. We need the face of God shining on us to be whole and healthy, but his light can't reach us when we're covered up in our sin.

It feels desperate, but the reality is there is no place too dark for God's grace to light up. All we have to do to be released from the covering of sin is to ask God to take it away. We can't do it ourselves, but he is faithful to forgive us as soon as we ask. God will turn around the moment you call out to him, and he'll replace your grubby old sin blanket for a new covering of clean light. Asaph was right that we can only be saved by God's grace. We can't save ourselves.

What are you covered in right now? Draw or write a description of the blanket you're wearing now and the one you want God to replace it with when he turns his face to shine down on you.

Psalm 126

Read Psalm 126. This is what happens when God takes away our sin. We may shed some tears because there will be consequences for our sins, but the ultimate punishment is taken away. Our hearts aren't held down by the weight of it anymore once God lifts it off of us. Like theses exiles returning to Jerusalem, we will be light and filled with laughter and joy and gratitude for the things that God has done for us.

We can have the deepest peace if we will let God rescue us. Our brokenness will reap rest for our souls if we offer it to God. Our every action will reap a consequence, be it for good or bad.

What are you sowing right now, and what will it look like at harvest time?

 Write or draw what your harvest will look like right now. Do you need to change how and what you plant?

Chapter 9 – Repeat as Necessary

I am always shocked to find that depression or anger or denial have crept back into my life. I feel somewhat betrayed by my emotions when one of those "old" demons haunts me; after all, I dealt with that several stages ago, didn't I? I've accepted my circumstances, and I've moved on with my life, so why is grief rearing its ugly head again? Like so many other things (fashion, history, home décor...), grief is cyclical rather than lineal. And I don't think it ever goes away – we just feel it more or less at any given moment.

I used to feel overwhelmed to repeat a stage of grief – like I was sucked into a black hole and this would be the time I couldn't recover and climb out. The early years were exhausting, especially when some new pain cut through my barely healing scabs. On good days, I felt like I avoided touchy subjects, peering over at the black hole and telling myself I wasn't going back in, but I knew I was too close for that to be the truth. Time and healthier coping skills have finally put some distance between me and the black hole. On occasion its gravity overtakes me still, but I know now that I won't be lost in oblivion.

As I've grown stronger and spent quality time with a therapist, I've learned that there are patterns that can trigger a relapse in sadness or depression. When I stay honest with myself about how I'm feeling, I can evaluate what led to an angry outburst (I mean, it's never really life or death if the toddler doesn't cooperate with toothbrushing – it only feels like my head is going to explode.) and trace it back to its source. Sometimes the images of pregnant people and lovely families with multiple children on social media are filling my heart with resentment instead of gratitude for my friends. Almost always, I'll come to realize that I've been neglecting some of the things I know I need to do to keep my mind healthy. When I see the pattern, I can be intentional about getting the help I need to get back on track and to keep depression brain in check.

Anniversary dates can sneak up on you. I knew for the first five or so years after our first pregnancy loss that April 1 would be a horrible time for me since it was the due date of our first baby. As the date approached, even if I wasn't actively noting it, my temper would get shorter, my stress level would jump, and I'd be dragging through every day looking for an excuse to go back to bed.

Holidays can also be abysmal, especially the first few years after the loss of a loved one. The first Christmas season after we lost that first pregnancy was torturous for me. I had always loved Christmas shopping and decorating, and I was struggling to not kick people in the shins from Thanksgiving until after the New Year. I had expected to be a glowing pregnant person in Christmas sweaters, but instead I was still having to tell people who had missed the news that we lost the baby. Christmas continues to be hard for me, even though years have passed and our daughter brings new joy to the season. I still struggle most years; I still miss the wonder and joy I used to have every Christmas.

Now I know what dates are obvious trigger points, so I work ahead of those times to prepare for more self-care and down time and avoid giant events that I know are going to be hard to deal with. I cut myself some slack when the crazy expectations I had in my head don't pan out quite the way I planned. I tend to overestimate the amount of things I can put on my schedule and actually complete, and this tendency gets worse with stress. When I catch myself over planning, I stop and make myself leave spaces on the daily planner. One of the best things to do is to take a break and go spend time with a friend; have coffee or dinner and give yourself some space to decompress. Maybe schedule something nice like a massage, or go see a movie you're excited about. We need to be careful not to jump into avoidance for too long, but it's good to give yourself some time without all the pressure.

As you walk through your grief, don't be discouraged when you find yourself back in an old and hurtful stage. It is a normal part of the journey to loop around; grief is more of a scenic journey than a direct route. It will feel impossible to take one more step some days, especially when you feel like you should have already moved on and overcome the thing that's tripping you up again. The good news is that God travels with us through every loop, vortex, abyss, and black hole. You don't have to drag yourself along – just rest in the knowledge that God is always holding you in his mighty hands. God's hands are infinitely strong and tender, and you are safe resting there.

Grief is an unpredictable journey, full of chaotic emotions and revolving stages. The one constant is that God is your foundation, the one true rock to cling to and build on. You'll be able to navigate better through the stages of grief with time and reliance on God as your one true constant. You can trust that your weakness and vulnerability are being developed into strength when you let God direct you. It feels like absolute malarkey when someone tells you that while you're in the throes, but it's true nonetheless.

You are stronger than you know. Feel free to question that with zeal. And then examine your journey to date. We humans tend to remember negative experiences and emotions more vividly than the positive ones, but that doesn't mean there aren't positive things happening to us even when life feels miserable. It's important for us to notice and remark on the positive things.

Make it a daily practice to write down at least three things that God provided for you that day and then thank him for those. I know it seems trite and overdone to count your blessings, but it's a solid mental health tool. It's a good reminder when we fall back into depression or bargaining or anger that God is in control and that he is always taking care of us. If you document it in a journal, you'll be able to go back and look at God's provision for you when you're having trouble remembering what you have to be thankful for.

Another practice to add to a daily gratitude journal is to challenge every thought to make sure it lines up with the truth of God's word and character. For example, one of my common "oh woe is me" thoughts sounds something like this: "What is so wrong with me that God won't give me the children I've asked for? Look at that woman who's on drugs and doesn't even want to be pregnant! God must not love me." Of course in hindsight I can see that those thoughts are so much crockery, but they *feel* true in the moment. I've grown enough through my grief that God doesn't let me live in that moment of crockery for more than a second. He tells me to shine his light on that thought and see if it holds up to truth. The truth is I am a sinner saved by grace who is dearly loved by my creator and who has been given more than I deserve.

I still loop through stages of grief, but each loop finds me stronger when I allow God's truth to challenge my thoughts and when I allow his peace to hold my heart steady. I can recognize the signs of the cycle more quickly and equip myself to handle it. It's important to never ignore what you're feeling; acknowledge it and air it out so that you can process it rather than repress it. When we ignore or deny our emotions, they'll find a way to seep out somewhere – and that never ends well. Express your emotion but don't allow the feeling to become your truth – only God can be that foundation, and our emotions will lie. (I may *feel* like Batman sometimes, but if I jump off a building, I'm going to break at least one bone.) Whatever we accept as truth must stand up to the standard of God's word. I can assure you that very few of my grief emotions or depression brain thoughts ever test out as truth when I take time to examine them.

I hope that if you've read this far, you've realized that there wasn't ever a simple straight-line growth in the Israelites' relationship with God. Even David, the man after God's own heart and an anointed king of Israel, didn't grow from strength to strength. He experienced times of closeness with God and personal success, and then something in his life would hold him back, maybe even push him completely away from his goals.

David never stopped coming back to God, no matter what happened, and that sets a clear example for how we can handle life. It will never be perfect, and we will never stop experiencing grief, but we can always return to Jesus and find him waiting with open arms and peace for our souls. You may repeat any and every stage of grief, but you should also repeat coming to Jesus for healing.

Psalm 27

Psalm 27 is a perfect example of repeating cycles while still holding tightly to faith. We see David starting out with an affirmation of his faith in God's salvation, which is the only foundation to build on that will never crumble. God is the only immovable, unshakeable rock to start from when everything else is falling apart. Like David, start with what you know to be true and work from there. There are a lot of wonderful things to digest in this psalm, but my favorite part is verse 8: *"My heart has heard you say, 'Come and talk with me.' And my heart responds, 'Lord, I am coming.'"* *(NLT)* Oh how my heart clings to this verse! God is saying, "Come sit and have coffee with me, and tell me what's going on." Just have a chat. Two old friends sharing time and space. This is God's offer to develop your relationship with him no matter what stage you find yourself in or how many times you've repeated it.

Can you spot emotional cycles in this psalm?

Can you spot emotional cycles in your life?

Practice sitting down with God for a chat. Draw or write about what that is like and how it strengthens your relationship with God. What effect do you see having regular friendly talks with God will have on your cycles through stages of grief?

Psalm 89

Read Psalm 89. It doesn't end the way I thought it would. The first 37 verses are nothing but uplifting praise; then the last 15 are desperation. How often have you felt like things were finally improving, you were growing and feeling lighter, and then suddenly your feet get knocked out from under you? It happens to all of us, and Ethan the Ezrahite saw it happen to the family line of David. I wonder if this psalm was all written at the same time, or if Ethan started his psalm writing on a good day only to have everything go to pieces on him before he could finish the song.

The most important thing that Ethan shows us through his psalm is that we must have a strong foundation. When our legs get cut out from under us, we're going to fall, and what we land on is of utmost importance. If our foundation shifts to ourselves – to what we can accomplish in our own strength – we're going to fall a lot farther before we stand up again. The coping mechanisms we choose that aren't based on God lead to nothing good for us when left unchecked: food, alcohol, drugs, shopping, anger...

Ethan's foundation was faith in God's promise, so it was the first thing he turned to when he fell. If you are completely honest with yourself, what is your foundation? Right now, I can honestly say I'm anchored firmly in God, but I have used food, shopping, and a tendency to revel in being angry and mean – all of which ended badly for my physical and emotional health, not to mention damaging relationships with everyone around me.

Use words or pictures to describe your foundation as it is and as you want it to be.

Psalms 57 and 59

Read Psalms 57 and 59. Both of these are psalms of David written about times when his life was immediately threatened by Saul. If you're a note reader, you may have noticed that both of these were written to be sung to the same tune. What I noticed about both of these songs is that the stanzas alternate between fear and calling out to God for rescue and then courage that comes from trusting God to be who he says he is and to do what he says he'll do.

Even if we heal and move on from an episode of grief, life will continue to happen. We'll either experience another loss or continue to feel the effects of one great loss, or both. Life isn't static, and neither is our emotional health. We must continue our efforts to grow and heal in both easy and hard times. The good news is that God isn't going anywhere – he's always ready to comfort us and save us.

If we think of our life as a song, it has more than one verse; it may have a chorus and a bridge; it has a pattern of repeating themes even if those themes are changed a bit each verse.

Imagine what the song of your life looks like. This episode of loss is only one verse in your life song.

What verse are you on now?

What do you think the next verse will be?

What is the chorus that you keep coming back to after every verse?

Chapter 10 – Shine Your Light

As you heal and come to terms with your loss, you will begin to feel lighter and happier. You just keep breathing and putting one foot in front of the other for a while, and one day, you'll be surprised that you feel "normal" and you're laughing more than you're crying. One of my favorite poems is called "Surprised by Joy" by William Wordsworth. (Have you ever heard of a more aptly named poet? I have been jealous of that last name from the second I heard of him in school.) In "Surprised by Joy," Wordsworth describes being surprised by something joyous and then turning to share it with the one he loved, and lost. The poem concludes with him feeling that this joy was painful both for happening without his love and for reminding him anew of his loss. I thought I understood this poem when I studied it in school, but I barely cracked it then. Now I have lived it, walked intimately through those lines and felt the jumble of emotions that must have inspired Wordsworth to record them.

As we feel lighter, we initially tend to feel guilt and shame for feeling happy when we think we should be feeling sad. That will fade, and it's important for you to know that you can let go of the guilt and pain so you can embrace the joy when it comes. Jesus wants you to have abundant life – to be filled to overflowing with his love – and God promises his people a hope and a future. I do not believe that this means you can pray yourself happy or rich or healthy. God answers prayers in miraculous fashion all the time, but I don't believe the idea that we can ask for anything and receive it – if we just believe hard enough – is biblical... or especially healthy to anyone's psyche. What God promises us through prayer is to give us what we ask for when it aligns with his purpose and plan. He promises to reveal himself to us through prayer. But he doesn't promise us all wealth and health all the time. I trust that this means God has only my best interests at heart, and I can lean in to him. I trust that guilt and shame are not part of his plan for anyone's hope or future, and Jesus invites us to bring him our burdens and trade them for his easy yoke.

So lay down the pain and the guilt as you go, and take up the light and the joy as they come. I say this like I am an expert. I honestly have no idea how to lay down my burdens; I am terrifically horrible at this particular spiritual discipline. In my practice of it, I imagine boxes or luggage tagged with each burden, and I imagine setting them down like a Christmas present at Jesus's feet. I tell him about it and why it's too heavy for me to carry, and I ask him to remind me that I can't carry it around anymore when I try to take back my boxes.

Another way I love to do this in my prayer life is to physically hold up my hands together, like I'm holding the burden out as I pray about it, and then to open my hands and rest them, palms up, on my lap to signify that I have released that petition to God and will sit quietly and listen for him to guide me. I didn't invent that physical gesture for prayer – it's something I learned in a college small group, and it's borrowed from a Quaker prayer tradition. Those are things that help me think about what it means to let go of something I feel and to give it to God. I'm far from perfect at living this out, but I'm getting better at it as I practice.

As we experience more joy, share it with God. This seems silly since he's the giver of the joy, right? But he wants to hear your praises. He loves to hear you sing and laugh. If we know that God collects every tear we shed in a bottle, what do you think he does with our laughter?

Shine your light when you feel it so that it can grow and make the inevitable dark moments more bearable. Shine your light to show God that you are grateful for his provision and his love. Shine your light so that you can be a light for someone else experiencing a dark night of their own. Share your joy when you find it, and it will multiply.

The old saying that what you feed will live and what you starve will eventually die is true in our faith and emotional health. If you focus on the good and true the most, you will have less time to wallow in the bad. As you focus more on light, you'll want more of it and will have lessening desire for darkness.

The psalms are rich in some of the most exuberant praise for God you will ever find. Let's read Psalms 8, 19, 24, 29, 47, 63, 84, 95, 96, 100, and 150. Rather than analyze each psalm independently, we're going to write our own psalm using these as a framework. As you read each psalm, I encourage you to read it several times and savor it. Feed the light growing in your soul. Make some notes or sketches from each psalm of the words and phrases that resonated the most with you. To write your psalm, I will get you started with each line, and then you fill in the words that come from your heart. There is no need to rhyme or worry about grammar – just write down the song in your heart.

A Psalm of Joy by:

O Lord, your name is

The stars in the sky proclaim your

Who am I that you would

You have made

And it is

The Lord is

The Lord is

The words of God are

And his voice

Come, everyone, and

Because God

I will praise you with

I will shout

Come, let us

Let the heavens

Praise the Lord in

Praise him with

Chapter 11 – Tell Your Story

This may sound like the previous chapter title, but this is more about sharing your experience. As you develop and heal from your loss, share your story with someone. Begin telling "safe" people like your family and friends, but don't stop there: tell more people around you as you feel more comfortable with the words and the vulnerability of relating your story. There are several reasons this is an important thing to do.

First, God calls us to be his "witnesses." A witness in court merely testifies to what they know about the case at hand; that's all God is asking us to do. Share your story of how he works in your life with everyone around you. I used to think my story was boring. I was a good kid who rebelled very little and grew up to be a decent adult. I've never smoked, never been drunk, and have only had sex with my husband. Boring.

But my story is amazing. God kept me from all kinds of trouble and protected my heart because he knew what I would experience later. I only survived my grief and depression because I have a foundation of faith to build on. I wouldn't have found a reason to stay here on earth if I didn't know that God is true, that God loves me, and that he will heal me completely one day in heaven.

Not only did I survive grief and depression, but I am also beginning to thrive and to know again what abundant life is. God doesn't need us to defend him or to prove his existence – he can do that on his own – but he wants us to faithfully share how he moves and works in us. That simple act of obedience is also a wonderful act of worship every time you tell your story.

Second, putting words to your emotions and your experience is powerful. It allows you to identify and name what you feel, and that awareness in turn allows you to work on healing painful emotions and fortifying positive emotions. Words are powerful: God spoke the universe into existence. Speaking your experience of grief out loud helps you process what's important to your experience and filter it into a narrative. The more you tell your story, the more control you feel over it and the more self-efficacy is restored. I have already told you about the first time I shared in perfect context the abbreviated version of our miscarriages and felt like it was just history. The person I was talking to exclaimed about how sorry he was, and I could honestly tell him, "It's just part of our story now." The sting had lessened so much that I no longer felt like I should speak in hushed tones to convey the sadness inherent in our loss. I could just tell the story and move on. Rather than feeling like the losses were the defining experience of my narrative, I was defining their place in my life as a touchstone for God's work in my life.

Third, tell your story because you never know who needs to hear it. Statistically, one in four women will experience a miscarriage. Anecdotally, less than half of them will talk about it. Not everyone needs to talk a lot about a loss, but most of the time people don't want to share something sad or extremely personal because they're afraid no one will understand, and they'll add the pain of rejection to the pain of loss.

Whatever your story is, someone needs to hear it. God wants to use your story to encourage someone, to draw them to him, and to bring glory to his name. *Your* story.